# IMAGES of America
# SHORT NORTH NEIGHBORHOOD

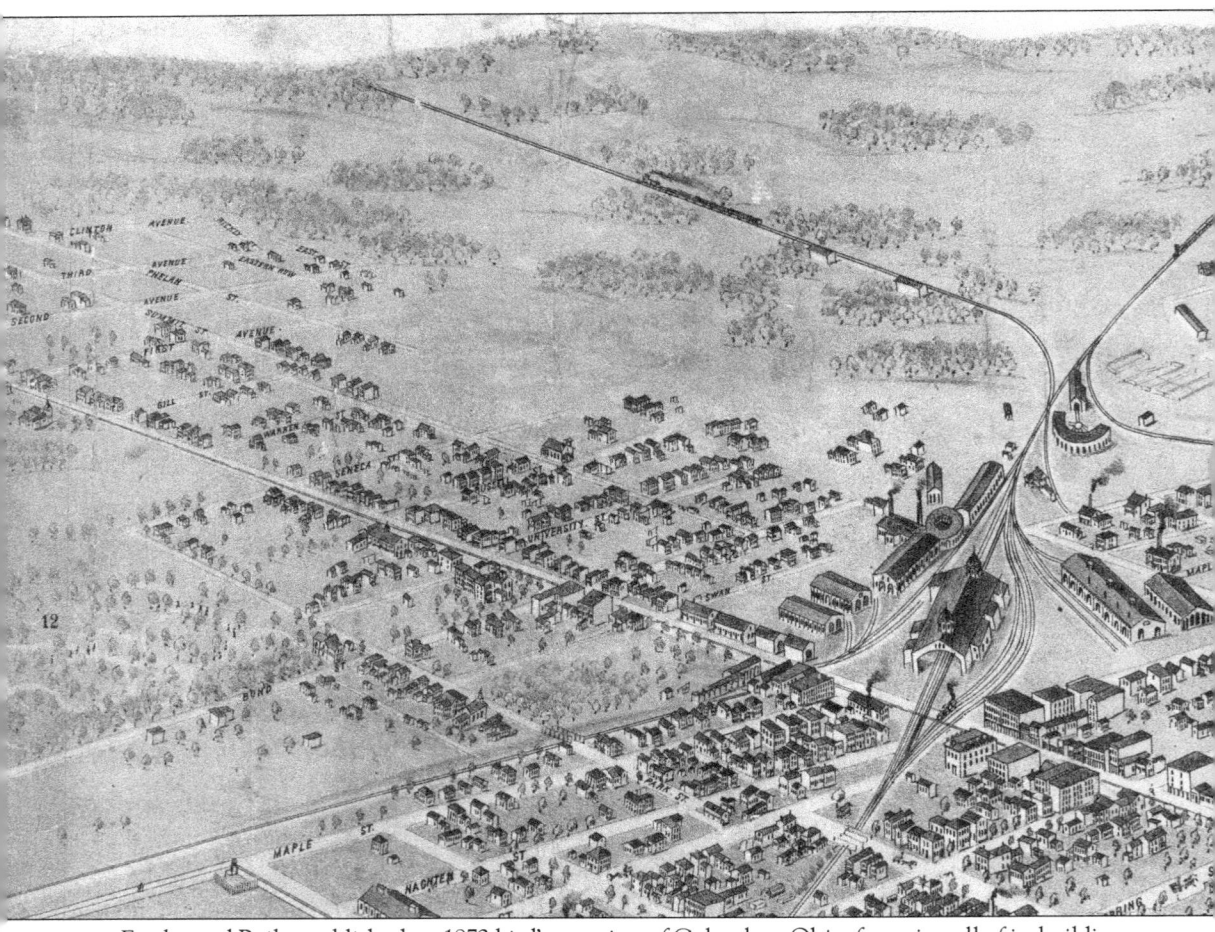

Fowler and Bailey published an 1872 bird's-eye view of Columbus, Ohio, featuring all of its buildings. This section of the map looks northeast and includes much of what would become Italian Village. Most of the rail lines lead into the depot at lower right in the image. Goodale Park, at left in the image, is marked by the number 12. (Courtesy of the Library of Congress.)

ON THE COVER: Children and adults line North High Street around Third Avenue as they anticipate the approach of the 1966 Thanksgiving parade. The annual event was sponsored by Lazarus Department Store and followed a five-mile route south from East North Broadway to Town Street. (Courtesy of the Columbus Metropolitan Library/Columbus in Historic Photographs.)

# IMAGES of America
# SHORT NORTH NEIGHBORHOOD

Nick Taggart

Copyright © 2020 by Nick Taggart
ISBN 978-1-4671-0456-2

Published by Arcadia Publishing
Charleston, South Carolina

Library of Congress Control Number: 2019949050

For all general information, please contact Arcadia Publishing:
Telephone 843-853-2070
Fax 843-853-0044
E-mail sales@arcadiapublishing.com
For customer service and orders:
Toll-Free 1-888-313-2665

Visit us on the Internet at www.arcadiapublishing.com

*For Michele, my best friend and traveling companion*

# CONTENTS

| | | |
|---|---|---|
| Acknowledgments | | 6 |
| Introduction | | 7 |
| 1. | 1850–1899: Beginnings | 9 |
| 2. | 1900–1949: Development | 31 |
| 3. | 1950–1979: Decline | 69 |
| 4. | 1980–Present: Redevelopment | 93 |

# Acknowledgments

It takes a village to preserve the history of a neighborhood. Ground zero for that preservation in my city is the Columbus Metropolitan Library. My coworkers in Local History and Genealogy all deserve recognition for their work and dedication in digitizing and archiving the images that appear in the library's My History digital collections. Thanks to Angela O'Neal, Russ Pollitt, Aaron O'Donovan, Julie Callahan, Scott Caputo, Chuck Cody, Loraine Wilmers, Lindsay Hunter, Michelle Brown, Judith Zawodniak, Charlotte Graham, Christopher Shanley, Nicole Sutton, Faith Mascari, and Kim Siphengpheth.

I also want to thank the following people and organizations that contributed images and enthusiasm: Jocelyn Probasco of the Godman Guild for her trust and generosity, Aimee Briley of the Columbus Historical Society, Wendy Wise of the Grandview Heights Public Library, Doreen Uhas Sauer of Columbus Landmarks, Brenn Waldman-Hinderliter of the Harrison West Society, and Matthew Adair and John Krygier, whose excellent work on the Engaging Columbus Project can be found at engagingcolumbus.owu.edu.

I want to especially acknowledge Dan Brewster, owner and manager of Prologue Bookshop, who proposed the idea of a book on the Short North; Margaret Marten, editor and publisher of the *Short North Gazette*, who led me to this project; and Sandy Wood for his assistance and, more importantly, the incredible role he played in making the Short North what it is today.

A special thank you to Terry Sherburn for his generosity of time and ready willingness to share his encyclopedic knowledge of the Short North.

And, finally, a huge thank you to my wife, Michele Reinhart, for whom I am eternally grateful for her support, suggestions, and editorial skills.

# Introduction

Ask five people who frequent the Short North area to draw its boundaries, and they might produce seven different maps. Their answers may depend on how those being surveyed interact with the area. Do they live or work there or only occasionally visit it for entertainment? For the purpose of this illustrated history, the boundaries will be defined as the CSX railroad tracks on the east, Goodale Boulevard on the south, the Olentangy River on the west, and on the north, King Avenue west of High Street and Fifth Avenue east of High Street. This area includes the business district of North High Street and is surrounded by the residential neighborhoods of Italian Village, Victorian Village, Harrison West, and Dennison Place.

The Short North is an attractive and thriving part of Columbus with an enviable mix of historic residential architecture ranging from stately Queen Anne mansions and Italianate homes to more modest accommodations. This vibrant commercial and arts district of unique galleries, varied restaurants, and eclectic shops is housed in its own historically significant buildings. It would be easy to forgive a recent transplant to the city for thinking it was always this way, but the Short North was crumbling in the latter half of the 20th century, and nothing was guaranteed about the revitalization of either the residential or commercial areas. In 1975, the cover story of the debut issue of *Columbus Monthly* was asking, "Will Victorian Village make it?" What gives the Short North its extra-special cachet is its long history of resilience and regeneration.

The area began as an outgrowth of what is now downtown Columbus. With the arrival of the railroad in 1850 and construction of the first depot on the city's northern edge, small businesses spread north, and industry developed on the fringes. Manufacturing brought factory workers, including immigrants from Germany, Italy, Ireland, and Wales, and, later, African Americans moving up from the South. Housing was constructed near the railroad and factories, and neighborhoods were born.

Sociology professor Roderick Duncan McKenzie published a study of life in Columbus in 1921. Even then, he observed that the city's neighborhoods were in a constant state of change—some improving, others declining. The Short North has continued to see its share of both trajectories. Challenges in the early 20th century included deteriorating housing conditions in some locations. The factories that brought jobs also brought dirt and odors. The prosperous who bought houses along Neil Avenue and around Goodale Park began moving out of the neighborhood, leaving many of their large homes to be divided into rental properties. The transitory nature of many tenants gave landlords little incentive to maintain their properties.

By mid-century, the city began to take notice, but solutions to the problems were often accompanied by dictates to "destroy the village in order to save it." Hundreds of families were displaced during the "slum clearance" of the 1950s, when homes were razed on 118 acres; much of the land was cleared to make way for the construction of an innerbelt expressway.

The following decade saw the creation of the Dennison Avenue Conservation Project, which was proposed to stem the deterioration of an area bounded by Fifth and First Avenues on the north and south and High Street and Neil Avenue on the east and west. With federal assistance, the project helped provide homeowners with tax credits and low-interest loans as incentives to improve their properties. However, part of this "conservation" effort involved razing 178 homes and relocating 190 families. In 1973, the city created neighborhood commissions in Victorian Village and Italian Village, giving them architectural review authority. This action put safeguards in place to support further preservation.

While revitalization was turning a corner throughout residential streets, it was slower to occur along North High Street. Already, the strip had gone by various names at various times. In the beginning, when it was little more than the area north of the railroad depot, it was called the North Side. As the city continued to grow, it became the Near North Side to distinguish it from city boundaries expanding even farther north. Around the 1960s, police dispatchers began referring to the high-crime territory as the Short North, as it was "short" of the University District and "north" of downtown. In the following decades, as entrepreneurs made tentative steps in the North High Street corridor, business owners embraced the name as a rebranding tool. According to Maria Galloway, the owner of pm gallery, "The Near North was a location; the Short North, more of an attitude."

That attitude persisted in a vision of what the Short North could be even when it was surrounded by evidence of blight and decay. It is not an overstatement to describe those early developers and business owners as brave pioneers. In the midst of boarded-up and falling-down properties, despite the prevalent crime, these folks paved the way toward the creation of a rejuvenated neighborhood known for its diversity and tolerance, free spirit, and charm.

As conditions improved, word spread that something special was happening in the formerly depressed neighborhood. New inhabitants were enticed by the safety and walkability of the residential streets, and people living outside the neighborhood were attracted to the exploding number of cultural events and entertainment opportunities. A cooperative multigallery art exhibit held in early 1984 was so successful that it soon became a monthly event and was christened Gallery Hop the following year. Independence Day 1984 was also the first year the Doo Dah Parade wound its way through the Short North. ComFest made the move to the neighborhood in the early 1980s, first to a parking lot across the street from Goodale Park, then, a few years later, to the park itself. The annual Columbus Pride Parade always includes the Short North in its route. And in 1999, the Columbus Italian Festival relocated its annual three-day celebration to the grounds of St. John the Baptist Catholic Church in Italian Village.

The Short North has changed greatly in the past 30 years. It is not the same neighborhood it was five years ago—or even one year ago. It is not going to be the same neighborhood five years from now—or even next year. Challenges are ongoing in areas such as historic preservation, development, increasing rents and property taxes, high-profile chains versus independent businesses, and parking—always parking, but if the recent past is any indication, the Short North will continue to meet those challenges with innovation.

A visual history is limited by the availability of images that have survived, but I hope this book spurs the memories of longtime residents, business owners, and habitués of the Short North and inspires them to record their own histories. For those new to the area, I hope this book serves as an introduction to the rich heritage of the Short North. Welcome to the neighborhood.

# One

# 1850–1899

## Beginnings

Forty years after the 1812 founding of Columbus, what is now known as the Short North area was still mostly forest and farmland bisected by a rough road called the Columbus-Worthington Pike (later renamed High Street). All that was soon to change.

The Columbus & Xenia Railroad arrived in 1850 and allowed passengers to travel by rail all the way to Cincinnati. A year later, rail connections to Cleveland were established. The city's first depot was constructed on what was then the north edge of town, where the Columbus Convention Center now stands. Its location spurred development in a northerly direction. Land began to be subdivided, and housing for railroad workers began to appear. By 1862, most of the area south of Fifth Avenue between Dennison Avenue and the eastern boundary of today's Italian Village had been annexed to the city.

In the 1870s, the railroad to Athens was completed, allowing coal and iron ore to be easily transported from southeast Ohio, spurring the growth of industry. Two corridors of manufacturing developed, essentially bookending the Short North. To the east, companies like Kilbourne & Jacobs and Buckeye Malleable Iron Company located northeast of the depot along the northbound rail lines. To the west, companies like the Columbus Pipe Works and the Smith Foundry set up shop on the eastern bank of the Olentangy River.

The factories were staffed with recent immigrants from countries like Ireland, Wales, Germany, and Italy. Inexpensive housing was constructed for these workers in communities such as Flytown, southwest of Goodale Park. The increase in population quickly led to the creation of ancillary businesses such as grocery stores and saloons as well as churches and schools.

Agricultural land was developed into residential streets and lots. William Neil's former private farm lane was transformed into the attractive, tree-lined Neil Avenue, where some of the city's affluent citizens lived in large Victorian homes. These burgeoning industrial communities formed the foundation for today's Short North neighborhoods.

This is the home of William Blackstone Hubbard, an early lawyer, statesman, and financier in Ohio. He had already served as an Ohio state senator and in the Ohio House of Representatives before he moved to Columbus in 1839. The house was built in 1850 by William A. Gill, who owned the property before Hubbard. Gill was the proprietor of W.A. Gill and Company, an agricultural warehouse and hardware store. When Hubbard purchased the house and surrounding property, it was considered to be in the country north of the city. As the city limits expanded northward, the property took on the address of 845 North High Street. After Hubbard died in the house in 1866, it served as home to subsequent generations of the Hubbard family and remained standing for over a half-century. Hubbard Avenue was named for this family. (Courtesy of the Columbus Metropolitan Library/Columbus in Historic Photographs.)

William Neil came to Columbus in 1818 and made his fortune in the stagecoach business. His 300-acre farm north of the city eventually became The Ohio State University. He subsequently purchased most of the land south of his farm (to the city limits) and between High Street and the Olentangy River. The lane leading to his home became Neil Avenue. (Courtesy of the Columbus Metropolitan Library/Columbus in Historic Photographs.)

One year after donating land for a park in 1851, Lincoln Goodale conveyed four acres at the corner of North High Street and Goodale Street (then Bond Street) to Capital University for a new campus. An Italianate-style structure was completed in time for fall classes in 1853. The school remained at that location for over 20 years before moving to Bexley in 1876. (Courtesy of the Columbus Metropolitan Library/Columbus in Historic Photographs.)

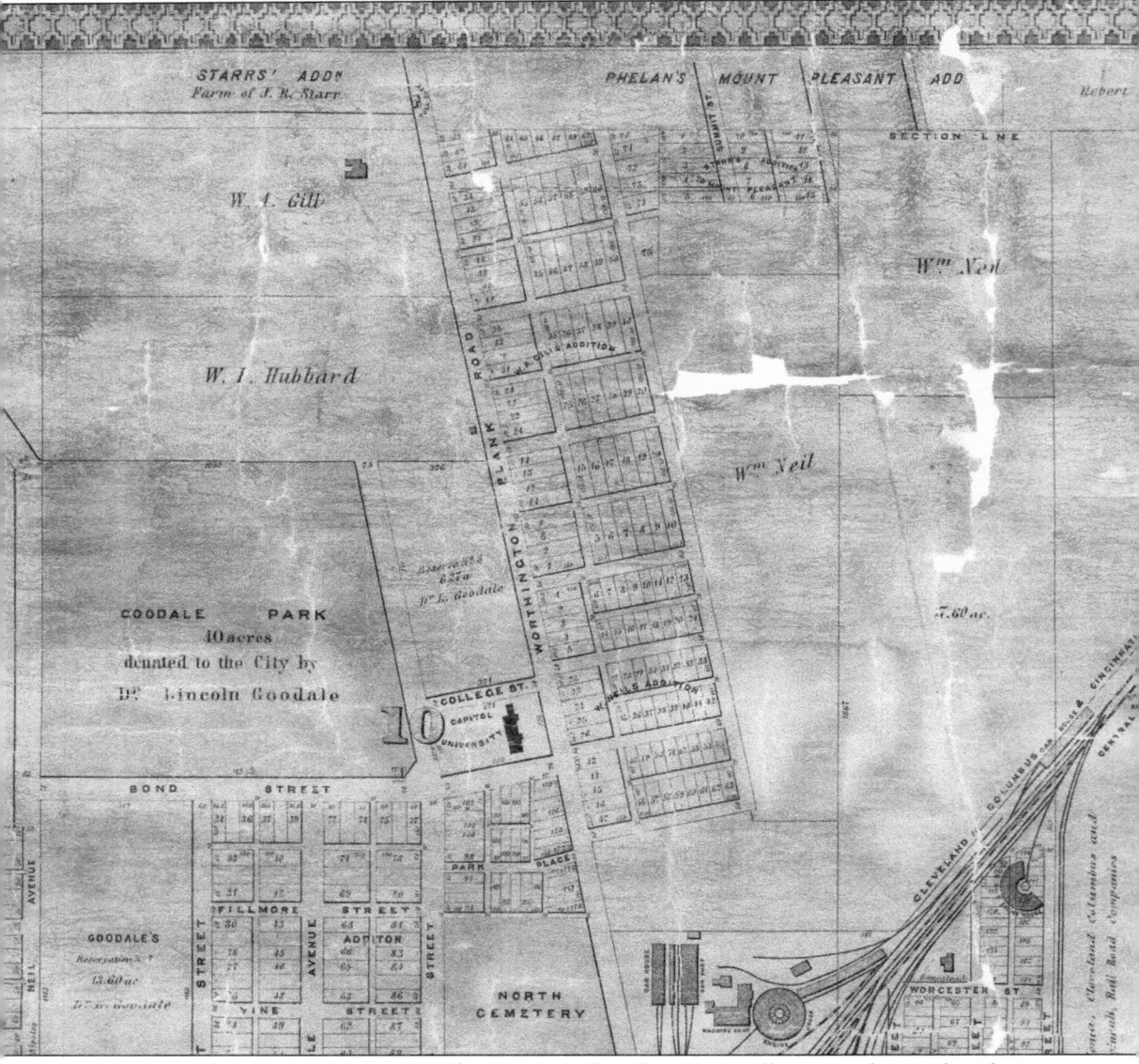

Lithographers Henry Hart and Dillon H. Mapother, from Louisville, Kentucky, produced a series of city maps in the middle of the 19th century. This is a portion of the 1856 map of Columbus, Ohio. It shows a section of the Short North when it was not much more than large tracts of undeveloped land. Property to the east of High Street, then known as the Worthington Plank Road, was beginning to be subdivided into smaller lots. Goodale Park was established in 1851, and Capital University moved to its High Street location two years later. Railroad tracks stemming from the depot are visible at lower right; that transportation link had a huge transformative effect on the Short North. The names of selected landowners represented on the map live on in the street names of present-day Columbus. (Courtesy of the Columbus Metropolitan Library/Columbus and Ohio Map Collection.)

Anne (Neil) Dennison was the eldest daughter of William and Hannah Neil. She was born in Columbus and spent her entire life in the city. She married William Dennison, who served as Ohio's governor from 1860 to 1862. Anne served for many years as president of the Columbus Female Benevolent Society and died at the age of 89. (Courtesy of University of Washington Libraries, Special Collections, POR826.)

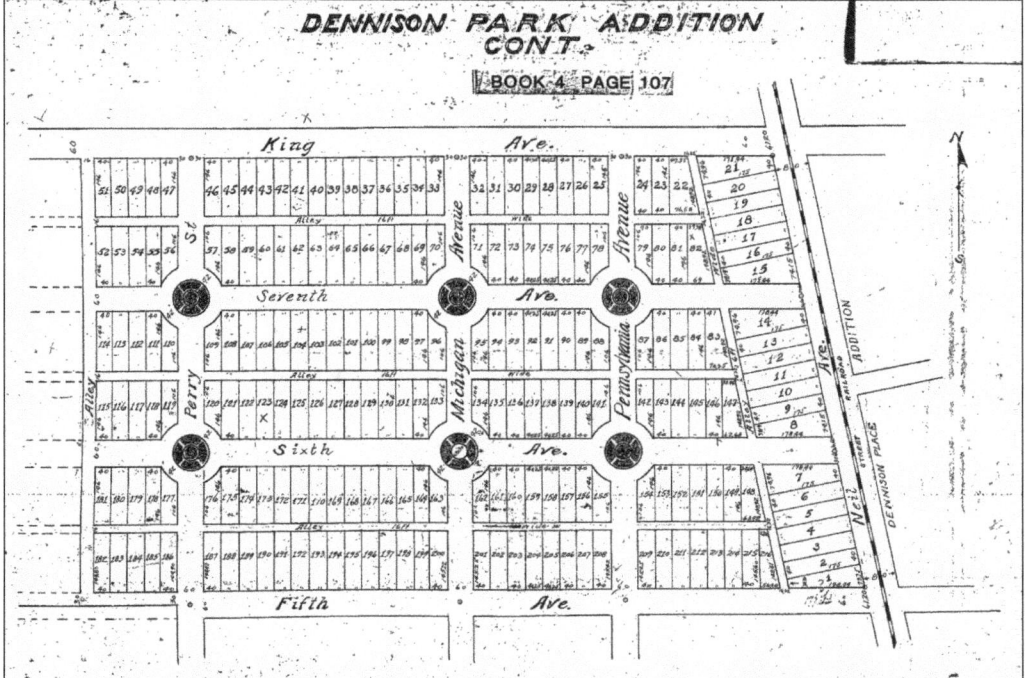

Anne Dennison laid out the Dennison Park Addition, also known as "the Circles," in 1888. It is believed she was inspired by famed landscape architect Frederick Law Olmstead. The addition is unique in Columbus for its rotary intersections that were meant to serve as neighborhood parks. The two Perry Avenue rotaries were lost during the expansion of the Battelle Memorial Institute. (Courtesy of the *Franklin County Recorder*.)

The Jeffrey Manufacturing Company, founded in 1876 as a partnership between Joseph Jeffrey and Francis Lechner, produced the world's first coal mining machines. It moved to 274 East First Avenue in 1888 and continued to manufacture machinery for the coal mining industry. After nearly a century under private family ownership, it was acquired by Dresser Industries of Texas in 1974. (Courtesy of the Columbus Metropolitan Library/Columbus in Historic Photographs.)

The Church of the Good Shepherd, at 41 Buttles Avenue, first held services here in 1887, two years before this picture was taken. The church was formed as part of a mission to serve railway workers and the poor. In 1928, it merged with the Mission Church of the Holy Spirit to form St. Stephens Episcopal Church. (Courtesy of the Columbus Metropolitan Library/Columbus in Historic Photographs.)

The C.M. Williams Building was constructed around 1889 at the corner of Kerr and Russell Streets. It was one of the first buildings to have a separate street entrance for each apartment. It was built of brick in an L-shape design with a large open arch that led into a central courtyard. (Courtesy of the Columbus Metropolitan Library/Columbus in Historic Photographs.)

The Fifth Avenue Elementary School at 210 West Fifth Avenue was constructed in 1886. For nearly 50 years, its 125-foot-tall tower was the highest point on the North Side, but it was removed in 1933 because it cost more to maintain the tower than it did to remove it. The school served neighborhood children for 90 years before being demolished in 1976. (Courtesy of the Columbus Metropolitan Library/Columbus in Historic Photographs.)

In 1873, William A. Neil built this house at 632 Park Street with a direct view of Goodale Park. It was later the home of George M. Peters, who formed the Columbus Buggy Company with his brother Oscar Peters and C.D. Firestone. The house, pictured here in 1889, was demolished in 1924 to make room for the United Commercial Travelers building. (Courtesy of the Columbus Metropolitan Library/Columbus in Historic Photographs.)

Lincoln Goodale donated land for a city park in 1851. He stipulated that the park "shall be forever kept and preserved, as a public park, or pleasure ground, for the free and common use of the inhabitants of said City of Columbus." The east lake, shown here in 1889, was constructed in 1875 for use by children accompanied by "prudent guardians." (Courtesy of the Columbus Metropolitan Library/Columbus in Historic Photographs.)

Nearly 40 years after Lincoln Goodale donated the land for the park that bears his name, he was honored with this bust by preeminent sculptor J.Q.A. Ward. The pedestal was designed by R.M. Hunt, who also designed the pedestal for the Statue of Liberty. This photograph was taken within a year of the monument's dedication in 1888. (Courtesy of the Columbus Metropolitan Library/Columbus in Historic Photographs.)

The northwest corner of High and Goodale Streets was desirable property. After Capital University moved to Bexley, the old university building was incorporated into the new Park Hotel. This 1889 image shows that the building also housed the Columbus Savings Bank and the Vienna Bakery Dining Room. (Courtesy of the Columbus Metropolitan Library/Columbus in Historic Photographs.)

Construction on this house at 749 Dennison Avenue was completed in 1888, a year before this picture was taken. It served as the home for husband-and-wife architects Elah and Isabel Terrell. Isabel designed the nearby northwest gate to Goodale Park. The house was demolished around 1947. (Courtesy of the Columbus Metropolitan Library/Columbus in Historic Photographs.)

This house at 773 Dennison Avenue is hard to miss with its beautifully cut stone. It sits diagonally across from the northwest entrance to Goodale Park and was the home of William H. Fish. His family owned the Fish Stone Company and the Fish Press Brick Company. Both firms supplied material for many of the neighborhood residences. (Courtesy of the Columbus Metropolitan Library/Columbus in Historic Photographs.)

A native of Wales, John R. Hughes came to Columbus and made his fortune in the trunk-making trade. He was also a cofounder of the Buckeye Buggy Company. His residence at 941 North High Street was constructed in 1870. This 1892 image features Hughes and his family posing outside the front entrance near a fountain. (Courtesy of the Columbus Metropolitan Library/Columbus in Historic Photographs.)

The house at 53 West Second Avenue was two years old when this picture was taken in 1892. This was the home of Frank L. Hughes, who took over the trunk-making business from his father, John. Frank met a tragic death in 1926, when he fell from an eighth-floor window. He was said to have been despondent over a recent diagnosis of impending blindness. (Courtesy of the Columbus Metropolitan Library/Columbus in Historic Photographs.)

The Third Avenue Methodist Episcopal Church was constructed on the northeast corner of North High Street and East Third Avenue. It was dedicated on January 3, 1869. Its mortgage was paid off two years before it was struck by a December 1896 fire. The congregation was successful in having it remodeled and rebuilt. (Courtesy of the Columbus Metropolitan Library/Columbus in Historic Photographs.)

Angelo Ross was a native of Italy who came to the United States in 1881. He and his wife, Elizabeth, ran a combination of businesses—including a hotel, saloon, and grocery store—from their property at 854 North Fourth Street. In 1905, they sold their property due to ill health. (Courtesy of the Columbus Metropolitan Library/Columbus in Historic Photographs.)

The property at 317 West Sixth Avenue, shown here in 1897, was the residence of John A. Kuster. Kuster was born in Newark, Ohio and attended college in Toronto, Ontario, Canada. He lived in Columbus for many years and was the editor and publisher of the *Catholic Columbian*. In 1905, he left for Denver, Colorado, where he was engaged in the real estate business. (Courtesy of the Columbus Metropolitan Library/Columbus in Historic Photographs.)

This residence at 1100 Neil Avenue was designed by architect Amos J. Solomon. He combined Romanesque and Corinthian styles of design. The building material consisted of pressed brick with buff stone trimmings. This image is from 1897. The house still stands at the northeast corner of Neil Avenue and West Third Avenue. (Courtesy of the Columbus Metropolitan Library/Columbus in Historic Photographs.)

It has been said that a man's home is his castle. Alfred L. Conklin's brick residence at 1237 Neil Avenue even featured a turret. Conklin served during the Civil War, attaining the rank of lieutenant. He later cofounded the business firm of Smith and Conklin. He died in 1901 after an operation for appendicitis. (Courtesy of the Columbus Metropolitan Library/Columbus in Historic Photographs.)

Dr. Charles A. Eckert, a dentist who graduated from Otterbein University and the University of Michigan, made his home on the southeast corner of Neil Avenue and West Fifth Avenue. This 1897 picture shows the house, which features pressed brick and heavy stone trimming, at 1260 Neil Avenue. Eckert was prominent in fraternal organizations. He died in 1920. (Courtesy of the Columbus Metropolitan Library/Columbus in Historic Photographs.)

The city realized it was in need of a large public auditorium when state conventions began selecting other cities for their gatherings. The old Park Rink, originally built in 1885 (for roller skating) at the northeast corner of Goodale and Park Streets, was extensively remodeled and opened as the Columbus Auditorium on June 24, 1897. These exterior and interior pictures were taken that year. The Columbus Auditorium hosted circuses, sporting events, and concerts, as well as the first Columbus Automobile Show, which was held on Christmas night in 1909. Less than two months later, just before midnight on February 18, 1910, the roof collapsed under the weight of accumulated snow. The crash could be heard for blocks. What remained of the building was razed. (Both, courtesy of the Columbus Metropolitan Library/Columbus in Historic Photographs.)

This 1897 photograph, looking southwest across the intersection of Dennison and Buttles Avenues, features a beautiful stretch of houses facing Goodale Park. The corner house (755 Dennison Avenue) was built in 1894 and is often called the Circus House because it belonged to Peter Sells, co-owner of the Sells Brothers Circus; it was designed by local architects Joseph Yost and Frank Packard. (Courtesy of the Columbus Metropolitan Library/Columbus in Historic Photographs.)

This 1897 image shows the southwest corner of Neil and West Fifth Avenues. All three houses were built and owned by Maj. R.W. Caldwell, constructed with pressed brick and stone trimmings, and included hardwood interior finishes of white walnut, ash, and hard pine. Caldwell lived in the house at 1265 Neil Avenue (located in the center of this photograph). (Courtesy of the Columbus Metropolitan Library/Columbus in Historic Photographs.)

A rough circular drive had been laid out in Goodale Park in the early 1860s. A decade later, the paths were improved. This 1897 picture was taken near the southeast entrance to the park. The boy on the left appears to be peering through the trees toward the Lincoln Goodale monument. (Courtesy of the Columbus Metropolitan Library/Columbus in Historic Photographs.)

The west lake was installed in Goodale Park in 1891. The boathouse, constructed four years later, also served as a veranda and a place for refreshments. This view from 1897 looks north from near Dennison Avenue and features a pedestrian bridge in the distance. The lake was removed in 1953. (Courtesy of the Columbus Metropolitan Library/Columbus in Historic Photographs.)

After a viaduct was constructed in 1895 over the railroad tracks in front of Union Station, traffic became much safer on High Street between downtown and the North Side. This 1897 photograph looks north on High Street from Goodale Street. Horses and buggies stayed to the sides to allow electric streetcars to travel down the center of the road. (Courtesy of the Columbus Metropolitan Library/Columbus in Historic Photographs.)

Hiram A. Pletcher was the oldest undertaker in Columbus when he died in 1917 at age 70. He came to Columbus in 1888 and established his business, pictured here, at 846 North High Street. He later moved the business to 1122 North High Street. Like other funeral directors, he provided ambulatory as well as funeral services. (Courtesy of the Columbus Metropolitan Library/Columbus in Historic Photographs.)

This is another picture taken at the corner of North High and Goodale Streets in the waning years of the 19th century. To the west of the Park Hotel is the old roller-skating rink before it was remodeled into the Columbus Auditorium. (Courtesy of the Columbus Metropolitan Library/Columbus in Historic Photographs.)

This 1898 photograph shows the residence of Charles Kinney at 754 Neil Avenue. Kinney was born in Kentucky but moved to Ohio in 1888 to serve as chief clerk to Ohio's secretary of state. He succeeded to the post in 1897 and served until 1901. He died in 1918. (Courtesy of the Columbus Metropolitan Library/Columbus in Historic Photographs.)

The house at 186 West Fifth Avenue, shown here in 1898, was home to Dr. Ola Hendrixson. At the age of 30, Ola Hendrixson moved to Columbus, where he studied medicine with his brother, who was a doctor. Ola Hendrixson graduated from the Columbus Medical College in 1885 and opened his own medical office on North High Street. (Courtesy of the author.)

Built in 1863 during the Civil War, Tod Barracks consisted of a series of temporary structures meant to house recruits and disabled soldiers. At least one of the buildings was later moved to 14–16 East Poplar Avenue and used for tenement housing. It looked presentable for a time but eventually became dilapidated and was torn down around 1911. (Courtesy of the Columbus Metropolitan Library/Columbus in Historic Photographs.)

G. William Baist was a surveyor and map publisher who produced large atlases for those performing real estate title searches and doing detailed building, subdivision, and infrastructure research. This 1899 map shows the southern section of what would become Italian Village between North High Street and the Big 4 Railroad. (Courtesy of the Columbus Metropolitan Library/Columbus and Ohio Map Collection.)

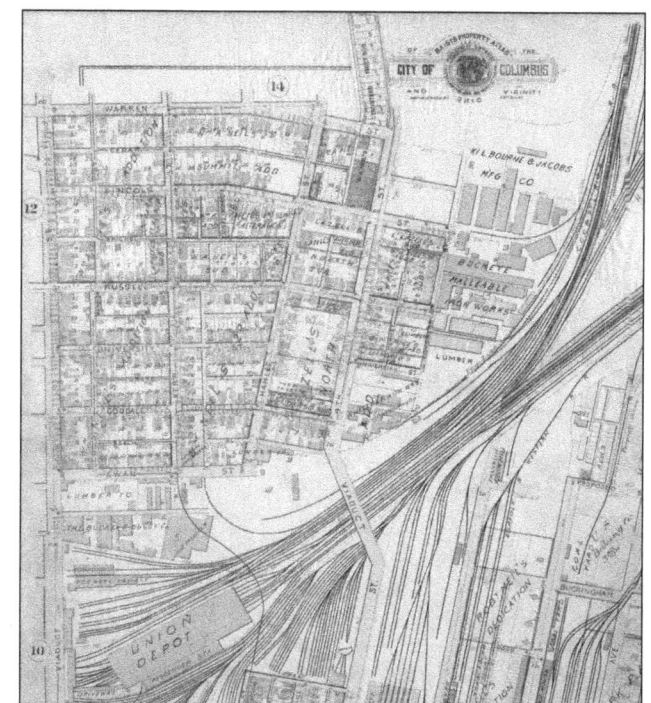

Maj. Wilbur F. Goodspeed founded the Buckeye Malleable Iron Company in 1886 and served as its president until his death in 1905. The factory at 219 East Russell Street manufactured small malleable iron castings for railroad cars. It closed in 1906, after the company changed its name to Buckeye Steel Castings Company and moved to a larger facility on Parsons Avenue. (Courtesy of the Columbus Metropolitan Library/Columbus in Historic Photographs.)

Construction on the Hubbard Avenue Elementary School, located at 104 West Hubbard Avenue, was completed in time for the 1895–1896 school year. The building holds the distinction of being the last Columbus school to contain a tower and dome. Due to increasing construction costs, such architectural features were abandoned for future schools. (Courtesy of the Columbus Metropolitan Library/Columbus in Historic Photographs.)

The May Terrace Apartment building extends a half block at 28–50 West Hubbard Avenue. It was designed by Columbus architect Richard Z. Dawson and completed in 1899. When this picture was taken, Hubbard Avenue was still a dirt road. In 1905, a six-room apartment at May Terrace could be rented for $25 per month. (Courtesy of the Columbus Metropolitan Library/Columbus in Historic Photographs.)

# Two

# 1900–1949

## Development

As the calendar pages flipped into the 20th century, the development of the Short North continued in an upward direction. The well-to-do continued to live in grand brick homes along Neil Avenue with distinctive architectural features like turrets, arched windows, and large porches. Manufacturers continued to prosper, which led to businesses needing more workers. In 1901, Jeffrey Manufacturing alone employed 800 people. With industry at its peak, the labor force expanded, and neighborhoods grew. Much of the Short North remained a stable middle-class residential community throughout the first half of the century.

Employment was not restricted to the large factories on both sides of the Short North. For example, West Goodale Street became a thriving commercial strip with small family-owned shops. A survey in 1927 included a restaurant, two pharmacies, three dry goods stores, two barbers, four confectioneries, a cigar shop, three billiard halls, a physician, and a dentist.

From 1915 to 1923, a major project widened North High Street so it could accommodate more traffic. Most of the older 19th-century building facades were removed from both sides of the street. The construction concluded with new zoning restrictions that set apart North High Street as a strictly commercial/retail district.

A new type of migration to the Short North took place in the years surrounding the First World War as African Americans left the South and settled in pockets east of High Street as well as in the Flytown area south of Buttles Avenue and west of Dennison Avenue. Flytown offered inexpensive housing and proximity to factory jobs for the new arrivals, as it had done for immigrants in previous years. Unfortunately, low-cost housing often equaled substandard housing. A 1933 federal survey of the area found "extensive dilapidation." In 1898, the creation of the city's first settlement house, the Godman Guild, led to an attempt to remedy some of the neighborhood's ills by offering health clinics and cultural resources for disadvantaged residents. Housing conditions in Flytown continued to worsen as the population increased, and landlords did nothing to maintain properties. This would lead to drastic corrective measures in later years.

Capt. Edward Fisher established his funeral home in 1870 at 1239–1241 North High Street; his son Edward E. Fisher took over the company upon the death of Captain Edward in 1893. The following year, Edward E. Fisher started the first ambulance service in Columbus—18 months before the city provided one. The firm went out of business in 1961. (Courtesy of the Columbus Metropolitan Library/Columbus in Historic Photographs.)

The Kilbourne and Jacobs Manufacturing Company incorporated in October 1881. Its factory at North Fourth and Lincoln Streets become well-known for the production of wrought steel and products such as barrows and earth-moving implements. The company was purchased by Case Crane and Engineering Company in 1922, which was, in turn, purchased by the Jeffrey Company in 1948. (Courtesy of the Columbus Metropolitan Library/Columbus in Historic Photographs.)

At the time this 1902 photograph was taken of Neil Avenue, a local newspaper reported, "Nothing in the history of the development of Columbus residence sections has been more remarkable than the growth of Neil Avenue from farms and woodlands to one of the most attractive residence thoroughfares in Ohio in the past 10 or dozen years." (Courtesy of the Columbus Metropolitan Library/Columbus in Historic Photographs.)

This c. 1905 view looking east across the Goodale Park east lake features the Protestant Hospital and Ohio Medical University. The combined buildings at 700 North Park Street provided an educational facility and 120 hospital beds. Protestant Hospital was renamed White Cross Hospital in 1923. The hospital closed after the 1961 opening of Riverside Methodist Hospital. (Courtesy of the Columbus Metropolitan Library/Columbus Memory.)

St. Francis of Assisi Church, at 386 Buttles Avenue, was designed by local architects Joseph Yost and Frank Packard. Bishop Watterson laid the cornerstone on September 1, 1895, and returned the following year to consecrate the building. A school opened on the property in 1905 and was staffed by seven nuns of the Dominican Sisters of St. Mary of the Springs. The city's urban renewal project at the end of the 1950s resulted in over one-third of the houses in the parish being torn down. The church lost over 250 families who had to relocate out of the neighborhood. The school closed in 1970 due to low enrollment and was destroyed by a fire three years later. The church, however, has survived, and in 2016, it celebrated its 120th anniversary. The day was celebrated with a Mass by Bishop Frederick F. Campbell. (Courtesy of the Columbus Metropolitan Library/Columbus in Historic Photographs.)

This view inside Boyd's Café, at 692 North High Street, shows not much has changed in saloon interior design in 100 years, perhaps with the exception of the swinging doors at the entrance. George W. Boyd worked as a freight conductor for the Pennsylvania Railroad for 34 years before trying his hand as a saloonkeeper. He operated his tavern from 1906 to 1912. (Courtesy of the Columbus Metropolitan Library/Columbus Memory.)

The gate at the northwest corner of Goodale Park has been called the William H. Fish Gate for the man who donated money toward its construction. He lived diagonally across from the entrance and, with his father, owned and operated the Fish Stone Company and the Fish Press Brick Company. The gate was designed by Isabel Terrell, who lived nearby on Dennison Avenue. (Courtesy of the Columbus Metropolitan Library/Columbus Memory.)

The Northern Hotel was "a dandy place to stay," according to the sender of this 1908 postcard bearing its picture. The view looks west on Goodale Street from North High Street. The hotel opened in 1878 under the name Park Hotel. The building was demolished in early 1958 to make way for the Goodale Expressway. (Courtesy of the Columbus Metropolitan Library/Columbus Memory.)

This French Second Empire–style house at 664 Park Avenue had many occupants. It was built in 1874 as a home for William A. Neil. It became the Parkview Sanitarium in 1902. After remodeling, it opened as the McKinley Hospital in 1921. Nearby White Cross Hospital used it as a dormitory for its nursing staff from 1927 to 1961. The building was demolished in 1967. (Courtesy of the author.)

Office of Capital City Dairy Co., Columbus, Ohio. Churners of World Famous Purity Butterine.

Capital City Dairy was founded in 1888. In 1919, it was renamed Capital City Products. It developed Butterine, perhaps the first all-vegetable margarine produced in the United States. It was sold under the brand name Purity and, later, Dixie. The Capital City facility at 525 West First Avenue employed many of the immigrants who lived in the nearby Flytown area. The company was acquired by Stokely-Van Camp Inc. in 1957 and changed ownership several times in the 1980s and 1990s. In 1996, the company merged with AC Humko. After operations closed in 2001, the buildings were razed, and nearly 300 homes were constructed in the place where the buildings once stood. (Both, courtesy of the Columbus Metropolitan Library/Columbus Memory.)

Capital City Dairy Co., Columbus, Ohio. Largest exclusive "First Quality Butterine" factory in the world.

GRACE U B CHURCH
FIFTH AVENUE    COLUMBUS, OHIO

The Grace United Brethren Church was founded in 1890 with 26 charter members. Construction was completed in 1894 on the church at 25 West Fifth Avenue, shown here in 1909. The name of the church changed many times over the following decades due to church mergers. The most recent was in the 1980s, when it was renamed New Life United Methodist Church. (Courtesy of Terry Sherburn.)

The Brethren Mission opened in 1912 at 471 West Third Avenue. It eventually became known as the First Brethren Church. Richard W. Morris, a longtime resident of the Harrison West neighborhood, was the church's last minister. After 30 years in the pulpit, Morris died in 2017, and the church closed two months later. (Courtesy of the Columbus Metropolitan Library/Columbus in Historic Photographs.)

Brethren Mission, Columbus, Ohio.

The Capitol College of Oratory and Music was classified as a school of "Expression and Dramatic Art." It taught classes in public speaking and singing and provided instruction for various musical instruments. Established in 1896 by Frank L. Fox, it used the building at 1076 Neil Avenue as its school from 1904 to 1955. (Courtesy of the Columbus Metropolitan Library/Columbus Memory.)

Anna B. Keagle opened the first social settlement house in Columbus in 1898 and began operating it out of rented buildings. Thanks to a $10,000 donation from local shoe manufacturer Henry C. Godman, a house was built at 470 West Goodale Street, and Keagle's settlement house was renamed the Godman Guild. It offered a variety of services, including music lessons, as shown here. In 1910, qualified music teachers offered over 1,500 music lessons. (Courtesy of the Godman Guild.)

A half century after troops were temporarily housed in Goodale Park at the beginning of the Civil War, the military once again set up camp in the park. In 1910, a strike by Columbus streetcar workers threatened to turn violent. After it was determined that the combined forces of the city police and county sheriff's deputies were not enough to control the situation, Ohio National Guard troops were called in to suppress the rioting and preserve order. An initial contingent of 2,000 troops arrived in the city on July 28. More troops followed two days later. Goodale Park housed Troop B and the 8th Infantry regiment. (Both, courtesy of Terry Sherburn.)

Frank Smith used these photographs as postcards that he sent to Ruth E. Smith in Lakeland, Ohio. They were taken in Goodale Park—in the vicinity of 661 Dennison Avenue—and feature some of the mundane tasks of the Ohio National Guard troops who were stationed in the park when they were not called to action. Less than two weeks after arriving on July 28, 1910, the troops were sent home; however, the worst violence occurred after their departure, including the death of a man who was hit by a stone. On the back of the postcard shown below, Frank wrote "Ruth, this is the way the soldiers get their meals like here. I think I'll go and see if I can get a supper with them too." (Both, courtesy of Terry Sherburn.)

41

The Godman Guild recognized the importance of physical activity in the development of children. It created the first supervised playground in Columbus in 1903. The City of Columbus followed its lead and took up the playground movement in 1910, creating a dozen supervised playgrounds of its own. In 1922, the Godman Guild added a gymnasium to its facility on Goodale Street. For many years, it was one of only two gyms in the city for young girls and boys and the only one where they could go no matter how little they were able to pay. (Both, courtesy of the Godman Guild.)

This c. 1911 view looking north shows tree-lined Neil Avenue north of Goodale Street. The houses on the left were razed a half century later for slum clearance, but most of the houses on the right still exist. The far-right edge of the picture includes a portion of the Neil Avenue Methodist Church at 610 Neil Avenue. (Courtesy of Terry Sherburn.)

Banners were stretched over North High Street in celebration of the Columbus Centennial in 1912. The Railroad YMCA building at left, on the northwest corner of North High and Goodale Streets was formerly the Park Hotel and the Northern Hotel. Just to the right of the YMCA building, the dome of the Capitol Clothing Company building is visible. (Courtesy of the Columbus Metropolitan Library/Columbus in Historic Photographs.)

The Billy Sunday Tabernacle was a temporary building erected at the northeast corner of Park and Goodale Streets to house a series of revivals held from December 29, 1912, to February 16, 1913. The Rev. William A. "Billy" Sunday was a popular national evangelist of the time. The tabernacle had a seating capacity of 12,000, with additional seats for a choir of 1,200. There were 95 meetings held during the period, sometimes three a day, and Sunday preached at all but two of them. The tabernacle was often full, and bad weather had no effect on attendance. The revivals resulted in over $44,000 in offerings and 18,333 reconsecrations and conversions. The tabernacle was razed soon after the final service. The photograph below shows people outside the tabernacle on Goodale Street. (Both, courtesy of the Columbus Metropolitan Library/Columbus in Historic Photographs.)

Construction on the first North High School began at 100 West Fourth Avenue in 1892. It was designed by Columbus architect Frank Packard. The three-story stone Romanesque Revival structure contained 14 rooms and cost $14,000 to construct. It was replaced in 1924 by a new building and renamed Everett Junior High School in honor of North High School's principal, Charles D. Everett. (Courtesy of the Columbus Metropolitan Library/Columbus Memory.)

This house at 98 Buttles Avenue, facing Goodale Park, was once home to O.L. Rankin, co-owner of Rankin, Price and Company Dry Goods. After William and Estella May Hutchinson donated materials to enhance the building, it was rechristened Hutchinson Hall and converted into housing for nurses from the nearby Protestant Hospital and Ohio Medical University. (Courtesy of the Columbus Metropolitan Library/Columbus Memory.)

The Plymouth Congregational Church at 43 West Fourth Avenue was constructed in 1895. This 1914 picture was taken three years after an addition was built. The congregation merged with First Christian in 1930 and became Congregational Christian Church. In 1949, it was renamed Plymouth United Church. The church disbanded in 1961, and the building was sold to Faith Baptist Church. (Courtesy of the Columbus Metropolitan Library/Columbus Memory.)

The Godman Guild sponsored clinics to which mothers could bring their babies to be weighed and examined. This c. 1915 photograph features mothers and their children outside the guild. The "BATH OPEN DAILY" sign on the left is a reminder of a service the guild provided at a time when home plumbing was not a given. The guild's facilities provided the first public baths in Columbus. (Courtesy of the Godman Guild.)

In May 1914, the Ohio Auto Sales Company opened this brick two-story showroom at 772-776 North High Street. The firm was composed of Charles Zimmerman and his two sons, Walter B. and Orr S. After Ohio Auto Sales moved out, for many years, the building continued to house companies related to car sales or repair. (Courtesy of the Columbus Metropolitan Library/Columbus in Historic Photographs.)

The Quad Stove Company, located at 76 East First Avenue, was established in 1901. It employed 40 people at its 30,000-square-foot facility. The company began by manufacturing cast-iron stoves but later added gas heaters, ranges, and army and camp stoves. The company was sold in 1958. (Courtesy of the Columbus Metropolitan Library/Columbus in Historic Photographs.)

This 1915 view looks south from the roof of Capital City Dairy on West First Avenue. In the center foreground is the Central Ohio Oil Company, located at 547 West First Avenue, with several storage tanks and railroad sidings. Also featured is a sawmill where a stack of cut trees is piled. (Courtesy of the Columbus Metropolitan Library/Columbus in Historic Photographs.)

Charles Benton Flagg was the first supreme secretary of the Order of the United Commercial Travelers of America (UCT). This memorial to him was dedicated in 1907 in Goodale Park. In 1949, it was moved across the street to the UCT headquarters. In 2012, it was returned to its original location in Goodale Park. This picture is from 1916. (Courtesy of the Columbus Metropolitan Library/Columbus in Historic Photographs.)

The Jeffrey Manufacturing Company was proud of the new electric lighting system it had installed on the shop floor in 1916, showing it off with before-and-after pictures in its company newsletter. This picture appeared on the June 1916 cover of the newsletter and looks north over the shop floor. (Courtesy of the Columbus Metropolitan Library/Columbus in Historic Photographs.)

The United Brethren Church at 33 West Fifth Avenue was the first of its denomination to be permanently established in Columbus. It was founded in 1890 with 26 charter members. Its original church building was partially destroyed by fire but was rebuilt and dedicated in 1916 as the Fifth Avenue United Brethren Church. (Courtesy of the Columbus Metropolitan Library/Columbus Memory.)

The Order of the United Commercial Travelers of America was chartered in 1888 in Columbus, Ohio. Eight traveling salesmen formed the society to provide accident insurance and other benefits for traveling salesmen (known as commercial travelers at the time) and their families. The house pictured above was built in 1873 and was the former home of William A. Neil, William Dennison, and George Merion Peters. It became the supreme headquarters of the UCT in 1903. It was demolished in 1924 to make way for a new headquarters, shown below. The building at 632 Park Street was sold in the 2010s and remodeled to house the Pizzuti Collection of art. (Both, courtesy of the Columbus Metropolitan Library/Columbus in Historic Photographs.)

The east lake was added to Goodale Park in the mid-1870s and has continued to be a popular gathering spot. In this 1920s photograph, two women pose next to the east lake. The winter conditions transformed the fountain into an interesting ice sculpture. White Cross Hospital is visible through the trees and beyond the line of cars on Park Street. (Courtesy of the author.)

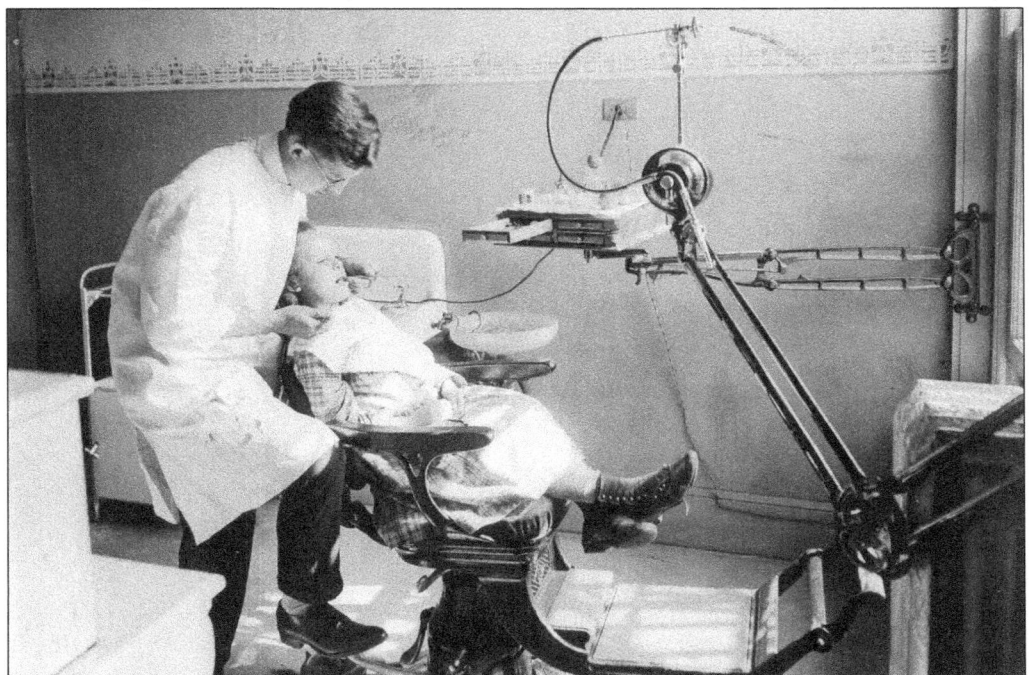

The Godman Guild provided a variety of services to the community and recognized the importance of good dental care. For two and a half days each week, dental exams were provided for children, as shown in this 1920s image. Staff also assisted adults with securing dental aid. (Courtesy of the Godman Guild.)

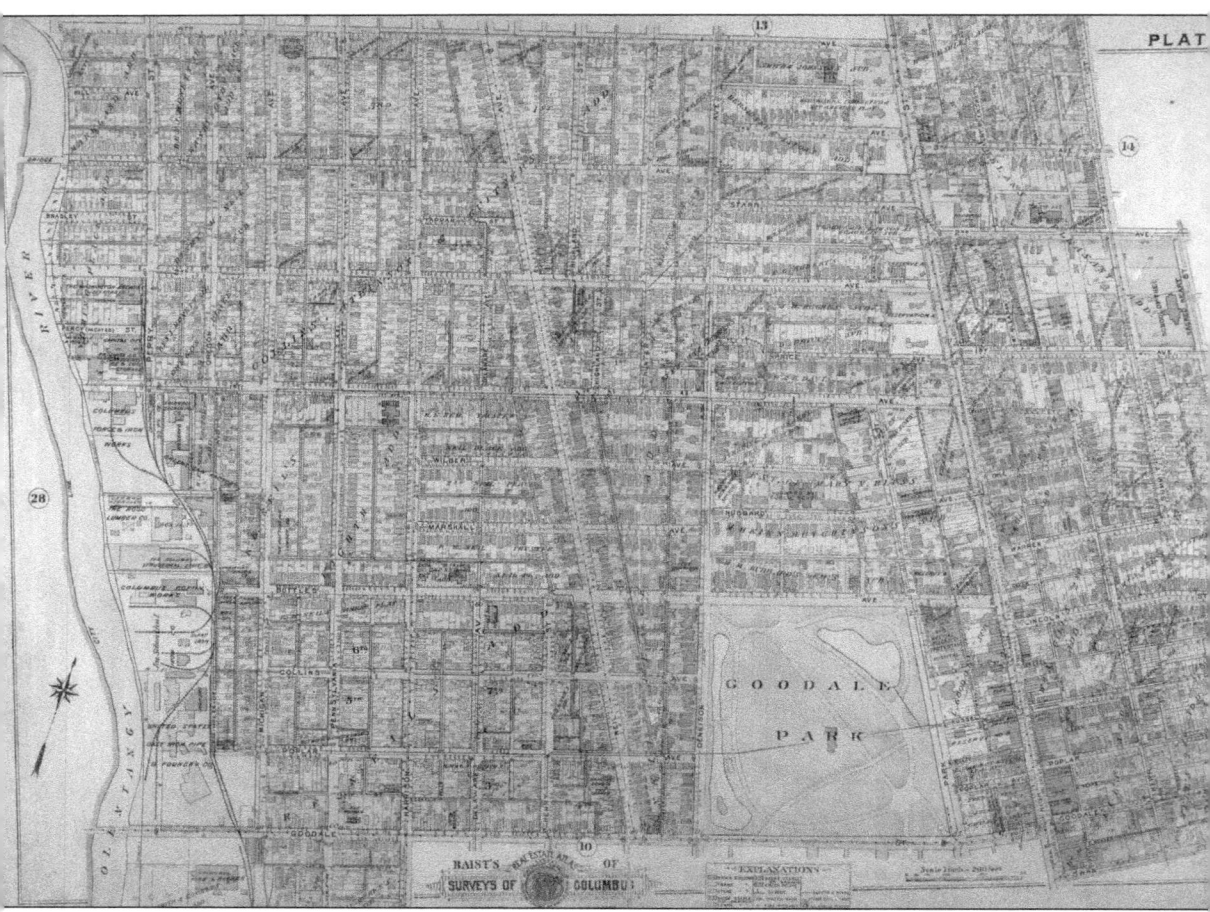

This 1920 Baist map features a huge swath of the Short North, including portions of the residential neighborhoods that would become Italian Village, Victorian Village, and Harrison West. The map is bordered by Goodale Street on the south and Fourth Avenue on the north, Hamlet Street on the east and the Olentangy River on the west. It offers a good pictorial example of how closely positioned the factories were to the homes of workers. The manufacturing corridor along the east bank of the Olentangy River went as far north as West Second Avenue and included such firms as the U.S. Cast Iron Pipe and Foundry Company, the Columbus Coffin Works, the Columbus Structural Steel Company, Columbus Forge and Iron Works, the Capital City Products Company, and the Washington Brewing Company. (Courtesy of the Columbus Metropolitan Library/Columbus and Ohio Map Collection.)

This 1921 photograph shows young women preparing food at the Godman Guild, which offered supervised classes in cooking, sewing, and craftwork. These classes, believed to provide important skills that would lead to self-respect, were well-attended. A 1910 report stated that many domestic science teachers in public schools throughout Ohio received their first work experience at the Godman Guild. (Courtesy of the Godman Guild.)

In 1888, Charles Zaner began teaching penmanship in Columbus. Legible handwriting was an important skill at that time, and his classes were popular. Seven years later, he teamed with Elmer Ward Bloser to form the Zaner-Bloser publishing firm. The company also operated the Zanerian College of Penmanship. The school moved to this building at 621 North Park Street around 1922. (Courtesy of the Columbus Metropolitan Library/Columbus Memory.)

In 1922, Forest Ira Blanchard wrote a master's thesis for The Ohio State University entitled "An Introduction to the Economic and Social Geography of Columbus, Ohio." His purpose was to study the racial and ethnic makeup of the city with a focus on how transportation in the form of railroads and roads shaped its development. In conjunction with his report, he took a collection of panoramic photographs that focused more on streets and neighborhoods than buildings or

events. This picture from the collection looks north on North High Street in the vicinity of Fifth Avenue. It exemplifies a little business center—a cluster of shops and restaurants surrounding a busy intersection where streetcar lines converged. (Courtesy of Engaging Columbus, Ohio Wesleyan University.)

This photograph looking north at High and Goodale Streets offers another example of a high concentration of businesses at the intersection of streetcar lines. Businesses include hotels, the Columbus Savings Bank, and The Gem theater. Also visible is the dome atop the Capitol Clothing Company at High and Russell Streets. (Courtesy of Engaging Columbus, Ohio Wesleyan University.)

This view of North High Street near Fourth Avenue shows businesses on the east side of the street and private residences on the west side. Forest Ira Blanchard believed this was partly explained by prevailing winds. He thought the west side received less blowing dust and dirt, which made it more attractive to homeowners. (Courtesy of Engaging Columbus, Ohio Wesleyan University.)

Another photograph from 1922 features a poorer residential area along East Fifth Avenue consisting of rowhouses and cheaply constructed apartments. The noise, dirt, and smoke of the nearby factories and railroad made this a less desirable area to live, but it was affordable for the working class, which had less socioeconomic power. (Courtesy of Engaging Columbus, Ohio Wesleyan University.)

This 1922 view along North Fourth Street features the sign and buildings of the Jeffrey Manufacturing Company, located at 274 East First Avenue. Forest Ira Blanchard used this as an example of the plants that formed an unbroken line of industry along the Big Four railroad lines north of Union Station. (Courtesy of Engaging Columbus, Ohio Wesleyan University.)

Italian native Emanual Abbruzzese immigrated to the United States at the age of 16. He was one of many Italians to settle in the Short North. By the early 1920s, he was the proprietor of Abbruzzese's Italian Food Shoppe at 390 West Goodale Street. The grocery store closed in 1959, when the city purchased the building through its slum-clearance program. (Courtesy of the Columbus Metropolitan Library/Columbus in Historic Photographs.)

Dr. Kinnis Fritter began construction on Greystone Court in 1907 but soon ran into financial problems. For the next decade, as work stalled, it became known as Fritter's Folly. The U-shaped structure was finally completed in 1921, just as the plan to widen High Street began. Twelve-foot sections had to be removed from each side and inched back to join the rest of the building. (Courtesy of the author.)

The Godman Guild organized athletic teams as part of its mission. It gave young people something to do while also building character and providing challenges for them to be their best. This Leaders Club team won the basketball championship in the 1924–25 season. From left to right are: (first row) Willie Boyer, Gus Young, "Chock" Ford, and L. Anderson; (second row) John Lipkin, coach Charley Cutchen, and L. Donaldson. (Courtesy of the Godman Guild.)

This photograph from the mid-1920s shows a group of 19 finely dressed young women assembled in front of the Godman Guild. Many are smiling. The guild organized clubs, meetings, and other social affairs for women while also providing health services, legal advice, and employment assistance. (Courtesy of the Godman Guild.)

Harry H. Shaw and D. Harvey Davis had already been in business for 17 years when they moved their mortuary to the house at 34 West Second Avenue in 1925. In a full-page advertisement in the *Columbus Dispatch*, they claimed it was the first funeral home in Columbus. The large residence featured three parlors, two showrooms, two reposing rooms, and an elevator lift and crypt. (Courtesy of the Columbus Metropolitan Library/Columbus Memory.)

This 1926 photograph of the 700 block of North Fourth Street was taken near Warren Street. The long building on the right was the assembly plant of the Jeffrey Manufacturing Company. Across the road, at 767 North Fourth Street, was the Columbus Metal Products Company. It was said that in 1926, 17,000 cars passed through this intersection each day. (Courtesy of the Columbus Metropolitan Library/Columbus in Historic Photographs.)

Jai Lai was a popular Columbus restaurant for over 50 years. It was founded by Jasper E. Wottring in February 1933 at 581 North High Street as a saloon and café. The interior views shown on this postcard date from the 1930s. In 1955, the restaurant relocated to 1421 Olentangy River Road. (Courtesy of the Columbus Metropolitan Library/Columbus Memory.)

Children gather on a front porch on Pennsylvania Avenue in this 1932 image. The purpose of the picture was to show the conditions of the street before sewer work began the following year. At lower right is advertising on the spare wheel of an automobile for the American-Italian Restaurant at 435 West Goodale Street. (Courtesy of the Columbus Metropolitan Library/Columbus Memory.)

It was laundry day on this pretty stretch of Oregon Avenue when this aerial photograph was taken on May 17, 1933. Cranes and equipment were in place for the impending sewer installation. About $2 million of public works program money was spent constructing sewers on the north and west sides of Columbus. (Courtesy of the Columbus Historical Society.)

This is another view of surface conditions as sewer installation work was started. This photograph, dated June 15, 1933, shows the northeast corner of Perry Street and West Second Avenue. The pickup truck next to the workers is City of Columbus car No. 61. (Courtesy of the Columbus Metropolitan Library/Columbus Memory.)

This photograph, dated July 22, 1933, looks south on Perry Street at West Third Avenue. The house on the southwest corner at 527 West Third Avenue (at right in the image) still exists. The sewer interceptor work conducted on Perry Street was not without danger; five workers died in a cave-in at Perry Street and West Fifth Avenue in 1934. (Courtesy of Doreen Uhas Sauer.)

This 1933 view looks north at the northwest corner of West Second Avenue and Oregon Avenue. The house on the left (502 West Second Avenue) was built around 1920. The duplex on the right (498–500 West Second Avenue) was built before 1900. Both structures still exist. (Courtesy of Doreen Uhas Sauer.)

This 1933 picture looks southeast across the corner of West Second Avenue and Oregon Avenue. The brick apartment block at 499–505 West Second Avenue was built around 1910 and still exists. Also featured in the picture is the duplex at 1036–1038 Oregon Avenue. It was built around 1921 and also still exists. (Courtesy of Doreen Uhas Sauer.)

The photographer who took this 1933 picture was standing at West Second Avenue and looking north up the alley just west of Oregon Avenue. Both of these buildings are still standing. The frame double on the left is 516–518 West Second Avenue. The brick house on the right is 510 West Second Avenue. (Courtesy of Doreen Uhas Sauer.)

This photograph looking northeast on West First Avenue was taken on August 14, 1933. The mounds of dirt at far right show that work on the sewer interceptor had already begun. The double in the middle of the picture sits at 526–528 West First Avenue on the alley west of Oregon Avenue and still exists. (Courtesy of Doreen Uhas Sauer.)

This photograph, taken February 16, 1933, looks north up Oregon Avenue from West First Avenue. The two brick apartment blocks on the left are over a century old and still standing. The addresses 514 and 516 faced West First Avenue, and 987 and 989 faced Oregon Avenue. (Courtesy of Doreen Uhas Sauer.)

Work had not yet begun, but the equipment was in place for the excavation of the sewer trench. The brick apartment building in this May 19, 1933, photograph sits at 987–989 Oregon Avenue. Rent for a five-room apartment at 989 Oregon Avenue was $12.50/month in 1933. (Courtesy of Doreen Uhas Sauer.)

A barricade was put up in the middle of the intersection at West Second Avenue and Oregon Avenue as a surveyor performed work in the area. This view from 1933 looks eastward and includes the Red and White store, a neighborhood grocery store located at 485 West Second Avenue and owned by William Dull. (Courtesy of the Columbus Historical Society.)

Most early Columbus beer breweries were located south of downtown, but one exception was the Washington Brewing Company, shown here in 1933, at 545 West Second Avenue. Construction of the brewery was completed in 1907. In 1912, it advertised its Bon-Ton brand of beer for 60¢ per case. (Courtesy of the Columbus Metropolitan Library/Columbus Memory.)

The first Northside Branch of the Columbus Public Library opened in this small space on May 21, 1940. The storeroom at 944 North High Street was renovated to be used as a library and leased from Henry and Donald Barricklow. It served the community for 18 years before moving into a larger location at 1100 North High Street in 1958. (Courtesy of the Columbus Metropolitan Library/ Columbus in Historic Photographs.)

The buildings at the southwest corner of North High Street and Fifth Avenue have not changed in 75 years—only the businesses are different. At the time this picture was taken in 1945, one could shop at the Miller Drug Company (1207 North High Street) or pick up a treat at Isaly's Ice Cream (1205 North High Street). (Courtesy of the Columbus Metropolitan Library/Columbus in Historic Photographs.)

This building at 1087 Dennison Avenue served as a medical facility after the Protestant Hospital was founded there in 1891. After the Protestant Hospital moved to Park Street, the house served as the Radium Hospital for many years, focusing on cancer patients. In 1938, it was renamed Doctors Hospital; the second-story veranda was added at that time. (Courtesy of the Columbus Metropolitan Library/Columbus Memory.)

# Three

# 1950–1979

## Decline

Noticeably deteriorating conditions in the neighborhood became more flagrant as the 20th century reached its midpoint. According to some, the rise of the automobile was a contributing factor, as it allowed those with means to move from the inner city to the suburbs. The less mobile were left behind in undesirable living conditions. Flytown was the poorest and most overcrowded area of the Short North. A 1950 federal census found that 25 percent of its dwelling units did not have running water.

In 1953, the Columbus Redevelopment Authority declared Flytown a blighted area. A report stated that 85 percent of its structures had six or more serious violations of building, fire, and/or health regulations. The area consisted of 384 structures containing 602 dwelling units in which 511 families lived. Three years later, a city bond issue approved clearance of an area totaling 118 acres, part of which would be set aside for the construction of the new Goodale Expressway. Demolition began in 1957.

The commercial strip along North High Street became more derelict as businesses closed and buildings became vacant. By the 1960s, the name "Short North" began appearing in reference to the area. Police used it as a handle for the area between downtown and The Ohio State University.

The city launched a rehabilitation program in the early 1960s to slow the decay of the residential area. Tax credits and government building grants were used to entice homeowners to improve their properties. This call for revitalization led to the formation of the Italian Village and Victorian Village Commissions in 1973. Another boost came in 1979, when the Near North Side Historic District was added to the National Register of Historic Places. The Near North Side Historic District boundaries were Goodale Street to the south and Eleventh Avenue to the north, the first alley west of North High Street to the east, and a zigzag line along Neil Avenue and Perry Street to the west. The corner had been turned toward serious redevelopment.

At the end of the 19th century, there were two major Italian communities in Columbus: Flytown and Milo. St. John the Baptist Church was purposefully located in the middle of those two neighborhoods at 720 Hamlet Street. Bishop Watterson appointed Father Cestelli to take charge of the needs of the Italian immigrants, many of whom worked on the railroads or in the nearby factories of Jeffrey Manufacturing or Smith Brothers Hardware. Cestelli oversaw the construction of the church, which was dedicated on September 18, 1898. A parade consisting of Catholic societies and Italian delegations marched from Chestnut and Fourth Streets to the church before the first Mass was held there. At the time of the church's opening, the congregation numbered 104 families. Since 1999, the Columbus Italian Festival has been held on the grounds of the church. The church is pictured here in the 1950s. (Courtesy of the Columbus Metropolitan Library/Columbus in Historic Photographs.)

Wayne Heber Shirley had been operating the Columbus Welding School when he purchased this building at 1122 North High Street in 1947. The property had formerly housed the Pletcher Funeral Home. Shirley changed the name of his school to the Shirley Trade School. He offered day and night classes in welding, body and fender repair, and shoe repair. (Courtesy of the Columbus Metropolitan Library/Columbus in Historic Photographs.)

The current King Avenue Methodist Church is the third church to stand on the corner of Neil and King Avenues. The first was a small stone church built in 1889. It was replaced in 1904 by a larger building, but it was destroyed by fire in 1918. The current church was dedicated in 1922. It is shown here in 1953. (Courtesy of the Columbus Metropolitan Library/Columbus Memory.)

The history of Sacred Heart Church, located at 893 Hamlet Street, dates to 1852 or 1853, when William Phelan donated the land to the diocese. Two decades passed before anything was built on it. In 1876, construction was completed on a building that housed a church as well as a school. Within two years of opening, enrollment at the school increased from 83 to 305. Additions were made to the buildings, but a growing congregation needed a larger church. On Thanksgiving Day, 1923, the new church, shown at left in the 1950s, was dedicated. Its Tudor Gothic style was designed by Robert Kraus of Akron. The Lady Chapel (below) was a small chapel to the left of the main chapel. This photograph was taken before it was remodeled in 1964. (Both, courtesy of the Columbus Metropolitan Library/Columbus in Historic Photographs.)

Haft's Acre was a popular entertainment spot in the neighborhood. The outdoor arena on the northeast corner of Park Street and Goodale Street drew a racially diverse crowd of male and female fans to the professional wrestling tournaments that took place beginning in 1927. The owner of the venue, Al Haft, was a former wrestler who became a wrestling trainer and a wrestling and boxing promoter. He founded the Midwest Wrestling Alliance and was one of the founding members of the National Wrestling Alliance in 1948. He primarily ran his operations from his base in Columbus. These photographs from Haft's Acre were taken by A.V. Shirk. (Both, courtesy of the Columbus Metropolitan Library/Columbus Memory.)

When this picture looking east on Poplar Avenue was taken in 1956, the street's days were already numbered. By the following year, these houses had been demolished to clear the way for construction of the innerbelt, later known as Interstate 670, that ran through this residential area. (Courtesy of the Columbus Metropolitan Library/Columbus Memory.)

This view looks east from the southeast corner of Goodale Park. The barrier, featuring advertising signs for Chrysler and Burger Beer, also formed a wall of Haft's Acre, the outdoor wrestling arena. Within a year after this photograph was taken on March 3, 1957, the wall and building beyond it were gone, making way for the Goodale Expressway. (Courtesy of the Columbus Metropolitan Library/Columbus Memory.)

These 1957 photographs feature the south side of Goodale Street. The houses and businesses along these blocks made up the main commercial strip of Flytown, an area that attracted European immigrants as well as migrants from the South. The above photograph looks east along West Goodale Street from the Godman Guild. The below photograph looks west from Goodale Park toward the intersection of Goodale Street and Dennison Avenue. Within a couple of years, all the buildings south of Goodale Street had been razed to make way for construction of the Goodale Expressway, later known as Interstate 670. (Both, courtesy of the Columbus Metropolitan Library/Columbus Memory.)

These photographs were taken on March 3, 1957. The above picture looks southeast from Goodale Park toward cars driving on West Goodale Street. The below picture also features West Goodale Street looking west from Park Street. The tallest building in the below picture is the Parkview Hotel, also known as the Lenox Hotel. All the buildings had probably been vacated by the time these photographs were taken. They were all gone within a year due to the city's slum-clearance program. The land south of Goodale Street was cleared for construction of the Goodale Expressway. (Both, courtesy of the Columbus Metropolitan Library/Columbus Memory.)

This 1957 photograph shows the east side of North High Street between Goodale Street and Poplar Avenue. It features the Prince Sandwich Shop (590 North High Street), the Hi-Goodale Recreation bowling alleys (594 North High Street), and the Stone Grill warehouse and headquarters (600 North High Street). All of these buildings were demolished to make way for the Goodale Expressway. (Courtesy of the Columbus Metropolitan Library/Columbus Memory.)

This 1957 view looks southwest at the intersection of North High Street and Poplar Avenue. The building housed Jai Lai for over 20 years before the popular restaurant moved to 1421 Olentangy River Road in 1955. The Ol' Place restaurant took its place. (Courtesy of the Columbus Metropolitan Library/ Columbus Memory.)

The Fourth Avenue Christian Church has been in the neighborhood since 1895. Its current building—located at 296 West Fourth Avenue on the northwest corner of that street's intersection with Neil Avenue—was dedicated in December 1926. The church belongs to the Disciples of Christ denomination. This 1957 postcard notes the minister, Albert O. Kean, who began his pastorage of the church in 1955. (Courtesy of the author.)

This photograph, dated August 1, 1957, shows the excavation work for the Goodale Expressway. The view looks northeast from the corner of West Goodale Street and Michigan Avenue. The dotted black lines were superimposed to show where an underpass would be constructed to allow expressway access under the neighborhood street. (Courtesy of Scripps-Howard Newspapers/Grandview Heights Public Library/Photohio.org.)

This photograph was taken inside Goodale Park on November 7, 1957. It looks southwest toward the intersection of West Goodale Street and Dennison Avenue. Demolition for the Goodale Expressway had already begun, as demonstrated by the empty space in the middle of the picture. The buildings on the left would soon be razed. (Courtesy of the Columbus Metropolitan Library/Columbus Memory.)

This is another photograph of West Goodale Street taken on November 7, 1957. This view looks east from the Godman Guild, located at 453 West Goodale Street. Construction on the new Goodale Expressway is well underway. The LeVeque Tower is visible in the background at far right. (Courtesy of the Columbus Metropolitan Library/Columbus Memory.)

This picture of the northeast corner of Park and Goodale Streets is dated December 27, 1957. The Haft's Acre outdoor arena had already been removed, and the remaining building would soon be razed to make way for the Goodale Expressway. The visible tower was part of the original Capital University, which was built in 1853 at North High and Goodale Streets. (Courtesy of Scripps-Howard Newspapers/Grandview Heights Public Library/Photohio.org.)

This photograph was taken on October 16, 1958, and shows the excavation and construction work on the Goodale Expressway. The view looks southwest from the Third Street viaduct. The top of the Yukon Building on North High Street is visible on the right. (Courtesy of Scripps-Howard Newspapers/Grandview Heights Public Library/Photohio.org.)

In 1958, the Northside Branch of the Columbus Public Library moved from its first location at 944 North High Street. This building at 1100 North High Street had previously housed the dry cleaning business of the Brown Dye House Company. The library vacated this location in 1975, when it moved to 1260 North High Street. (Courtesy of the Columbus Metropolitan Library/Columbus in Historic Photographs.)

This aerial view from 1959 looks northwest over the southern portion of the Short North and shows construction on the Goodale Expressway. The many railroad lines leading north out of the downtown area are evident in the lower portion of the picture. The Smith Brothers Hardware Company building at 580 North Fourth Street is near the lower-right corner. (Courtesy of Scripps-Howard Newspapers/Grandview Heights Public Library/Photohio.org.)

This 1959 photograph shows the Michigan Avenue Methodist Church at 1072 Michigan Avenue. The congregation was forced to move from Goodale Street due to the construction of the new expressway. The church began in 1868 as the Goodale Chapel, an interdenominational mission. It became a Methodist church in 1937. The stainless steel tower housed a historical bell brought over from the Goodale Chapel. (Courtesy of Scripps-Howard Newspapers/Grandview Heights Public Library/Photohio.org.)

This view looks southwest at the corner of West Fifth Avenue and Forsythe Avenue and was taken on April 17, 1963. The commercial brick building housed Saum's Cut Rate Store (247 West Fifth Avenue) and the 5th and Neil Washateria. The laundromat was equipped with 30 Westinghouse washers and 8 gas dryers. (Courtesy of the Columbus Metropolitan Library/Victorian Village Collection.)

Albert and Elsi Wildi ran a grocery store at 1085 Highland Street for over 25 years. A year before this picture was taken in 1963, a gunman tried to rob the small shop. Albert, who grew up on the South Side and called himself a "bullheaded Dutchman," pulled his own revolver and chased off the crook. (Courtesy of the Columbus Metropolitan Library/ Victorian Village Collection.)

This two-story brick home at 256 West First Avenue stood on the northwest corner of West First Avenue and Highland Street. The house was vacant by 1966 and razed after that. A house built in 1890 at 1001 Dennison Avenue was moved to this lot in 1980 and designated 933 Highland Street. (Courtesy of the Columbus Metropolitan Library/ Victorian Village Collection.)

Clifford B. Ferguson was a building contractor who lived at 1200 Neil Avenue. His office was just around the corner at 211 West Fifth Avenue, shown here on June 12, 1963. The building had already been abandoned and condemned when, three years later, firefighters from two companies battled a fire that destroyed the structure. (Courtesy of the Columbus Metropolitan Library/ Victorian Village Collection.)

This 1963 photograph shows the Lawson Milk Company's convenience store at 233 West Fifth Avenue just one year after it opened. It supplied the neighborhood with staples such as milk, bread, and eggs until 1968. The building stood vacant for a few years but later housed Reed Arts and Crafts and, beginning in 2003, Las Maravillas Mexican Market. (Courtesy of the Columbus Metropolitan Library/ Victorian Village Collection.)

This photograph from July 11, 1963, features two rarities that would be difficult to find today—a phone booth and an automated ice station. The City Products Corporation had large units scattered around the city. This one at 147 West Fifth Avenue, on the corner of Hunter Avenue, offered block, cube, and crushed ice 24 hours a day. (Courtesy of the Columbus Metropolitan Library/Victorian Village Collection.)

This three-story brick building once stood at 203 West Third Avenue. Apartments were on the upper floors, while the ground floor was used as a grocery store, a storeroom, a church, and the office for the KMS Building Products Company. This picture is dated August 1, 1963. The building disappears from city directories after 1966. (Courtesy of the Columbus Metropolitan Library/Victorian Village Collection.)

Ray Ashbrook began working as an attendant at this filling station at 103 West Fifth Avenue in the 1930s. He worked his way up to manager and eventually purchased the station. When this photograph was taken on August 29, 1963, it was known as the Ashbrook Shell Station. It closed three years later, and the building was razed. (Courtesy of the Columbus Metropolitan Library/Victorian Village Collection.)

West Fifth Avenue businesses were captured in a photograph dated August 29, 1963, that features the Fifth Avenue Barber Shop (133 West Fifth Avenue) and Bayles Auto Electric Service Company (137 West Fifth Avenue). Bayles sold its inventory in an auction in 1966 just before urban renewal led to the demolition of these buildings. (Courtesy of the Columbus Metropolitan Library/Victorian Village Collection.)

This commercial building on the southwest corner of Hunter and West Second Avenues housed a variety of businesses during its history, including a barbershop, shoe repair shop, beauty salon, confectionery, café, and food market. All had closed by the time this picture was taken on September 17, 1963. During the following decade, the building was razed and replaced with condominium units. (Courtesy of the Columbus Metropolitan Library/ Victorian Village Collection.)

This two-story brick home at 234 West First Avenue is one of the survivors in the neighborhood. It was over 60 years old when this photograph was taken on September 17, 1963. It was advertised in 1972 as "good rental property" and offered for sale by M.H. Meyer and Associates at a price of $9,000. (Courtesy of the Columbus Metropolitan Library/ Victorian Village Collection.)

Here comes Santa Claus—pulled by reindeer and a tractor in the annual Thanksgiving parade sponsored by Lazarus Department Store. This 1966 photograph looks north on North High Street from Third Avenue and features some of the Short North businesses of the time, including Kroger and Big Bear. (Courtesy of the Columbus Metropolitan Library/Columbus in Historic Photographs.)

This photograph, taken on April 16, 1968, looks south on Dennison Avenue from West Second Avenue. It shows the small office of Klinger's Sunoco Service station at 976 Dennison Avenue. Ralph F. Klinger, who owned the filling station for 30 years, passed away the year before this picture was taken. (Courtesy of the Columbus Metropolitan Library/ Victorian Village Collection.)

This 1970s aerial view looks west over Goodale Park. At the bottom is the empty lot on Park Street that provided free parking. Due to its rough surface and deep potholes, it was often compared to the surface of the moon. It disappeared in 1993, when ground was broken for the Victorian Gate apartment and condominium project. (Courtesy of the Columbus Metropolitan Library/David Lucas Collection.)

For over 50 years, an office and supply equipment store occupied 1037 North High Street. Eriksen's Inc. was the name on the building from the 1920s until 1970, when it was purchased from the parent company by a group of employees who renamed it Viking Business Equipment. The store closed in the early 1980s. (Courtesy of the Columbus Metropolitan Library/David Lucas Collection.)

Washmaid Laundry occupied this location at 245 West King Avenue for many years until 1972, when David L. Harris took over the operation and renamed it the Apocalypse Cleaning Emporium. It lasted a year before the business was put up for sale due to the owner's "other commitments"—the classified ad suggested the laundry service would make an "ideal husband and wife operation." (Courtesy of the Columbus Metropolitan Library/Columbus Memory.)

At 532 square feet, this may be one of the smallest houses in the neighborhood. It served as a grocery store for the first half of the 20th century. When this photograph was taken in 1973, its windows were boarded up, but a sign advertises the Mission Church of the Revival. It has since been rented as a unique three-room cottage. (Courtesy of the Columbus Metropolitan Library/Columbus Memory.)

Not much has changed—except the models of the automobiles—since this photograph was taken in 1974. The view looks northeast on Neil Avenue and features duplexes at 640–642 Neil Avenue and 670–674 Neil Avenue. Between them is the Sohio gas station, which later became a BP station, at 660 Neil Avenue. (Courtesy of the Columbus Metropolitan Library/David Lucas Collection.)

The grand house at 354 West Sixth Avenue, shown here in 1975, was designed by well-known architect Frank Packard and was the home of prominent grocer Charles Wheeler. Wheeler retired in 1908 after managing a successful downtown grocery store opened 56 years earlier by his father. He also built the city's first skyscraper, the Wheeler Building, at Broad and High Streets. (Courtesy of the Columbus Metropolitan Library/Columbus Memory.)

A man is tying an ottoman to the back of his bicycle in this 1977 photograph. This was a time when go-go bars were still common in the area, as shown by the sign for the Sly Fox Lounge at 711 North High Street. The Sly Fox opened in 1975 and was destroyed by fire in February 1978. Arson was suspected. (Courtesy of the Columbus Metropolitan Library/David Lucas Collection.)

Thanks to tax credits and government grants, homeowners in Victorian Village were motivated to make improvements to their properties. The improvements added value to the properties and attracted newcomers to the neighborhood. This photograph from 1979 shows two men on scaffolding performing maintenance on the exterior front porch roof at 682 Neil Avenue. (Courtesy of the Columbus Metropolitan Library/David Lucas Collection.)

# Four

# 1980–Present

## Redevelopment

By 1980, work toward halting the decay of the residential neighborhoods in the Short North was showing progress. A study conducted that year by the Victorian Village Society found that 24 percent of the buildings surveyed had been renovated or restored. The price of an average house had skyrocketed fivefold in eleven years—from $10,000 to $50,000.

Similar progress was being made in Italian Village. The Martha Walker Garden Club, formed in 1981 and made up of a dedicated group of resident volunteers, assisted in beautifying the neighborhood. The club's initial mission was to rid vacant lots of an abundance of trash and weeds and plant flowers, shrubs, and trees in the cleared lots.

Despite best efforts, the Short North ranked high in vice in the early 1980s. A local newspaper compared 1983 Columbus Police statistics and population figures and concluded that the Near North Side had more crime per capita than any other section in the city. That did not stop a few brave business pioneers from moving into the North High Street commercial strip. They were aided by forward-thinking developers, and key among them was Sandy Wood, who rehabilitated old properties with an eye toward how they could fit within the larger community. Wood enticed gallery owners to relocate to the area and helped plant the seeds that blossomed into the current arts district.

The area was given a new identity when the North High Street business owners began referring to the commercial strip as the Short North. In 1984, the same year as the first Doo Dah Parade, local art galleries banded together for a multigallery event that, by the following year, was rebranded the Short North Gallery Hop. Soon thereafter, ComFest, the annual festival of music, arts, and political activism, relocated to the neighborhood, followed by the Columbus Italian Festival. In 1996, Stonewall Columbus moved into its new center on North High Street.

The conversion from abandoned and neglected properties to trendy restaurants, chic shops, and rehabilitated homes did not happen overnight. The work, which continues today, has produced a gem of a neighborhood to make all of Columbus proud.

This aerial view from 1981 looks south over the Harrison West neighborhood. West Fifth Avenue appears at the bottom of the picture. The road running north–south through the middle is Perry Street. The Third Avenue Bridge, spanning the Olentangy River, is in the upper right portion of the picture. (Courtesy of Columbus Metropolitan Library/David Lucas Collection.)

This 1981 aerial view looks east across North High Street into Italian Village. A lot of unoccupied space is evident, but the following year, the block at Hubbard Avenue and Kerr Street would be converted into Italian Village Park and dedicated to Carl Proto, a former parks supervisor who died in 1981. (Courtesy of Columbus Metropolitan Library/David Lucas Collection.)

The First Avenue School was Sandy Wood's first large effort at redevelopment in the Short North. The school had been built in sections from 1873 to 1891 and closed in 1974. After refinishing the interior, rewiring, and replumbing, Wood repurposed the building into the First Avenue Office Center. It is shown here in 1983, the year it reopened. (Courtesy of Columbus Metropolitan Library/Department of Development Collection.)

When this photograph was taken in 1983, the future looked bleak for this two-story commercial building on the northwest corner of West Third and Michigan Avenues. The sign was all that was left of the Third Avenue Community Co-op, located at 444 West Third Avenue, after a 1978 fire caused an estimated $5,000 in damage. Recent renovations have given the building new life. (Courtesy of Columbus Metropolitan Library/Department of Development Collection.)

The Old Ice House had been closed for a few years when this picture was taken in 1983, but it had operated for decades, supplying ice for the neighborhood in the days before cheap refrigeration. The building was razed in 1989 to make way for a parking lot. The building on the left, at 1105 Pennsylvania Avenue, became Katalina's Café Corner in 2010. (Courtesy of Columbus Metropolitan Library/Department of Development Collection.)

The Michigan Market occupied the southwest corner of Michigan and West Third Avenues for many years. It was owned by Harold E. Johnston and his son David. When this picture was taken in 1983, Dave's Pizza operated at 1113 Michigan Avenue. The corner store was later renovated by Anton Wood, who operated Caffe Apropos there from 2004 to 2018. (Courtesy of Columbus Metropolitan Library/Department of Development Collection.)

The Michigan Avenue School, located on the southeast corner of Michigan and West Fourth Avenues, was constructed in 1904 and opened on January 4, 1905. The school served the community until 1976. After $1 million in renovations, the building reopened in 1981 as the Michigan Avenue Apartments, offering federally subsidized housing for senior citizens. (Courtesy of Columbus Metropolitan Library/Department of Development Collection.)

The Olentangy Management Company, a subsidiary of Battelle Memorial Institute, spent $22.5 million in the Harrison West neighborhood in the late 1970s and early 1980s. Its methods of revitalization were controversial at times, involving the demolition of houses, but it was also responsible for the construction of many "infill" homes, such as this one at 378 West Fourth Avenue, which is pictured in 1983. (Courtesy of Columbus Metropolitan Library/Department of Development Collection.)

When the Goodale Expressway construction led to the demolition of most of the buildings in Flytown, the original home of the Godman Guild was among the victims. The guild moved to a new building at 321 West Second Avenue in 1963; it is pictured above in 1983. The guild continued to provide educational, recreational, and other social services to the community. Land was purchased next to the building, and in the mid-1970s, it was converted into a community park containing a playground, shuffleboard and horseshoe courts, and a sunken basketball court (below). The park was named in honor of longtime guild social worker Bernadine Killworth after she retired in 1980. In 2002, the Godman Guild moved to its current location on East Sixth Avenue. The Second Avenue property was sold and converted into residential housing. (Both, courtesy of Columbus Metropolitan Library/Department of Development Collection.)

The Northfork Lounge, also known as the Northfork Saloon and Northfork Bar and Grill, served as a neighborhood hangout for about a decade in the 1980s and 1990s. Located at 1034 Perry Street, it was replaced by Outland, a music club that lasted nearly another decade. After Outland closed in 2004, the building was razed and replaced by condominiums. (Courtesy of Columbus Metropolitan Library/Department of Development Collection.)

This is an example of the kind of small businesses that were often found interspersed throughout residential housing. Shown here in 1983, the JR Body Shop was located at 576 West Second Avenue. Since then, the building has been converted into an apartment. It was included in the 2016 Short North Tour of Homes and Gardens. (Courtesy of Columbus Metropolitan Library/Department of Development Collection.)

This 1983 aerial view looking north features the remnants of Harrison West's industrial past. The Capital City Products plant still filled the area between Perry Street and the Olentangy River south of West First Avenue. Less than two decades later, the company, then operating as AC Humko, would close its doors. The buildings were razed and replaced by residential housing. (Courtesy of Columbus Metropolitan Library/Department of Development Collection.)

Sandy Wood's first High Street redevelopment project was this building at the northeast corner of North High and Lincoln Streets. When this photograph was taken in 1984, the coveted corner location of 714 North High Street was still occupied by Lincoln TV. The following year, it was Ritchey's at 714. More recently, it housed Jeni's Splendid Ice Creams. (Courtesy of Columbus Metropolitan Library/Department of Development Collection.)

One of the pioneer businesses in the revitalization of the neighborhood was the Short North Tavern, which opened in 1981. Shown here in 1984 at its original location at 660 North High Street, it later moved north a few doors to 674 North High Street. Owners John Allen and Gregory Carr were active participants in the promotion of the area. (Courtesy of Columbus Metropolitan Library/Department of Development Collection.)

Another pioneering business of the revitalized Short North was Functional Furnishings. Opened in 1976 by brothers Jeff and Matthew Unger, it was known for its funky contemporary furniture. It is shown here around 1984, when it occupied only a corner of the Yukon Building. It eventually filled the entire street-level space before closing in 2004 after 28 years in business. (Courtesy of Columbus Metropolitan Library/Department of Development Collection.)

It is sometimes difficult to imagine the vision required of a developer to see the potential in a rundown, deteriorated building. This c. 1983 view of the Carriage House building at 692 North High Street is obviously a "before" picture, as it features a closed furniture store and derelict storefronts. (Courtesy of Sandy Wood.)

This "after" picture from 1985 shows the results of Sandy Wood's renovation of the Carriage House. Putt'n on the Dog, a vintage clothing boutique, had moved into the spot at 682 North High Street. The Old Time Religion Hall at 700 North High Street is visible at far left. (Courtesy of Columbus Metropolitan Library/Department of Development Collection.)

This c. 1984 picture shows scaffolding on the northwest corner of Buttles Avenue and North High Street. The J&G Restaurant operated here for 35 years. After renovation, it reopened in 1988 as the J&G Diner. That restaurant was succeeded by Elements Grille in 2004, 8 Restaurant in 2007, and Black Olive in 2008. Bakersfield opened here in 2013. (Courtesy of Columbus Metropolitan Library/Department of Development Collection.)

The Garden, located at 1187 North High Street, began operating as a neighborhood movie theater around 1920. Its reputation became a bit tawdry when it reopened as a burlesque and adult movie house in 1975. Shown here around 1984 offering "classy nude dancers," it closed in 1986 as part of a plea bargain agreement after its operators were charged with promoting prostitution. (Courtesy of Columbus Metropolitan Library/Department of Development Collection.)

Featured in this photograph from the late 1980s is the storefront at the corner of High Street and Poplar Avenue. It housed Aardvark Video at 618 North High Street and Short North Dry Cleaners at 608 North High Street. It was threatened by demolition during the Interstate 670 construction but survived and later housed the Blick Art store and Callander Cleaners. (Courtesy of the Columbus Metropolitan Library/Columbus in Historic Photographs.)

The Columbus Foundation was established in 1943 as a public trust to serve Central Ohio's charitable needs. Battelle Memorial Institute donated this house at 1265 Neil Avenue to the foundation to serve as its headquarters. It functioned in that capacity from December 1982 until October 1988, when it moved to 1234 East Broad Street. (Courtesy of the Columbus Metropolitan Library/Columbus in Historic Photographs.)

When Kent Rigsby opened his restaurant at 698 North High Street in 1986, he was taking a chance on a neighborhood that was still quite rough. His was one of the first upscale dining options in the Short North. When Rigsby's closed in 2015 after a successful run of nearly 30 years, the neighborhood was home to more than 70 bars and restaurants. (Courtesy of the Columbus Metropolitan Library/Columbus in Historic Photographs.)

This building at 1088 North High Street housed various used-car lots in the 1960s and 1970s. In 1986, it became Prosort Incorporated, a professional mailing service. It served as the Short Stop teen center for a couple of years in the late 1990s and was then home to Byzantium, a bead store, for the first decade of the 21st century. (Courtesy of Columbus Metropolitan Library/Department of Development Collection.)

In 1985, six years after leaving her home in the Soviet Union with her husband and daughter, Isabella Grayfer opened Casa Isabella at 674 North High Street. Her Eurostyle store, seen here in 1986, featured contemporary furniture lines from countries such as the Netherlands, Italy, Belgium, and France. When Casa Isabella moved out of this location in 1988, the Short North Tavern moved in. (Courtesy of Doreen Uhas Sauer.)

This mural of the old Union Station arcade was painted by Greg Ackers on the north exterior wall of Aardvark Video at 618 North High Street. It was sponsored by Citizens for a Better Skyline and completed in 1987. It disappeared with the construction of Le Méridien Columbus, The Joseph hotel in 2014. (Courtesy of the Columbus Metropolitan Library/Columbus in Historic Photographs.)

The Ideal Furniture Company, located at 641 North High Street, spanned two periods of the Short North's history. The firm was in business from 1931 to 1987. The three buildings in which it was housed date to the last quarter of the 19th century. When Ideal ceased operations, Sandy Wood purchased the buildings and preserved the historic facades, including the eight-foot-tall windows. The center structure's metal front is unique to the Short North. The upper stories, which had been vacant for 15 years, were remodeled into apartments. Two art galleries and a dance studio were the first ventures to go into the commercial spaces. After renovations in the late 1980s, the buildings have housed popular dining destinations, with the opening of Lemongrass Fusion Bistro in the late 1990s and the Pearl restaurant in 2013. (Both, courtesy of Sandy Wood.)

The *Short North Gazette* debuted in 1987 under the title the *Fabulous Short North*. Founded by Tom Thomson, it began as a 22-page booklet. Thomson reveled in the compilation and publication of the periodical up to the time of his death in 2015. It continues to cover the people and events of the neighborhood as a bimonthly paper published by Margaret Marten. (Courtesy of Margaret Marten.)

This 1987 aerial view looks northwest and features the sprawling complex of the Jeffrey Division of Dresser Industries. The 33 buildings south of East First Avenue had been sitting empty for five years after a downturn in the coal-mining industry led to a reduction in the production of mining equipment. The buildings would be razed soon after this picture was taken. (Courtesy of Columbus Metropolitan Library/Department of Development Collection.)

This 1987 photograph features pm gallery, located at 726 North High Street, one of the first galleries in the neighborhood. Maria Galloway and Michael Secrest opened the art shop in 1980, selling an eclectic mix of original works ranging from paintings to pottery and glass. After a brief period at 1190 North High Street, the shop closed in 2018. (Courtesy of Columbus Metropolitan Library/Department of Development Collection.)

Children play on a swinging tire and other recreational equipment at the Fitness Cluster in Harrison West Park. The small park at 447 West Fourth Avenue is shown here in the 1980s. The Columbus Convention and Visitors Bureau awarded the park one of its City Beautiful Awards in 1988. (Courtesy of the Columbus Metropolitan Library/David Lucas Collection.)

Major Chord jazz club was owned by Columbus City Council president Jerry Hammond. It opened on New Year's Eve in 1987, after the former Old Time Religion Hall at 700 North High Street had been renovated by Wood Development. After Major Chord closed in 1989, two more music venues—Indigo 88 and 700 High—gave that location a try, but neither survived more than two years. (Courtesy of the Columbus Metropolitan Library/Columbus in Historic Photographs.)

Shown here in 1988, Chelsie's was just beginning a 12-year run as a popular venue for live music. Before Chelsie's opened, the building at 980 North High Street housed Dutch Café for a half-century, then Alice Faye's, then Duda's, and then was known more for drug raids and violence. Police reported 166 runs there in the first six months of 1986. (Courtesy of Sandy Wood.)

This aerial view of the Short North from 1988 looks northeast from Goodale Park. The east lake, or pond, is visible in the lower right corner. Quite a few of the vacant lots have since been developed into houses, businesses, and mixed-use projects. (Courtesy of the Columbus Metropolitan Library/Columbus Memory.)

This view of the east side of North High Street south of Fifth Avenue was taken around 1988. At far right is Gene's Furniture, owned by Paul Sporzynski. It had been operating at 1174 North High Street for only a few years. The building's previous tenant was Hoffman's Department Store, which closed in 1982 after 30 years in business. (Courtesy of Columbus Metropolitan Library/Department of Development Collection.)

Another c. 1988 picture of the east side of High Street shows the block between Third and Fourth Avenues. Michael's Goody-Boy, located at 1144 North High Street, was named for original diner owner Michael Pappas. Eva Ricci Mahaffey purchased the building at 1128–1130 North High Street in 1978 and, with her daughter Melanie, opened Mary Catherine's Antiques the following year. (Courtesy of Columbus Metropolitan Library/Department of Development Collection.)

The Fireproof Warehouse and Storage sign, shown here around 1988, has long been a neighborhood landmark at 1024 North High Street. The century-old building, with its 12- to 18-inch-thick concrete walls and vault-like rooms, provided storage for company records and household furnishings. Since 2011, when most of the operations were moved to another facility, other purposes have been sought for the building. (Courtesy of Columbus Metropolitan Library/Department of Development Collection.)

The southeast corner of North High Street and Fifth Avenue was long home to a hardware store. McDonald Hardware operated there in the early years of the 20th century before Ackers Hardware, founded by Charles H. Ackers, took over in 1921. The company was later owned by Paul H. Dortmund. Ackers is shown here around 1988, prior to its closing. (Courtesy of Columbus Metropolitan Library/Department of Development Collection.)

The Body Shop, located at 772 North High Street, was another building successfully renovated by Wood Development. The former automobile showroom was converted into retail space for galleries and shops. This 1988 photograph features signs along Warren Street for CR Obetz Gallery, Ace Gallery, the Fergus-Jean Studio, the flower shop Floristiks (run by Shelley Turf and Stephanie Gifford), and Portraits by Jeni. (Courtesy of the Columbus Metropolitan Library/Columbus in Historic Photographs.)

This building on the northeast corner of North High and Lincoln Streets was one of Sandy Wood's early redevelopment projects. In the 1980s, it housed Ritchey's at 714, an eclectic shop that sold coins, arrowheads and other memorabilia. It was owned by Doug Ritchey, who began business in 1980 at a neighboring coin shop at 716 North High Street. (Courtesy of the Columbus Metropolitan Library/David Lucas Collection.)

When this photograph of the southwest corner of North High Street and Fifth Avenue was taken around 1989, the Inn Town Restaurant had replaced the Golden City Restaurant at 1203 North High Street, but the Golden City sign still remained. To its north is the Presto Lounge, owned by Gus Stravelakis, and the Spirit Art Gallery, owned by Spirit Williams. (Courtesy of Columbus Metropolitan Library/Department of Development Collection.)

At the end of the 1980s, one could stroll down this stretch of North High Street and shop for a hidden treasure at Mary Catherine's Antiques (1128 North High Street), catch a bite to eat at Downtown Connection (1126 North High Street), and get a classic Sheaffer pen repaired at Vintage Fountain Pen Sales and Service (1124 North High Street). (Courtesy of Columbus Metropolitan Library/Department of Development Collection.)

The Gallery Hop began as a monthly event in 1984 to entice visitors to the galleries and shops of the Short North. In this 1989 photograph, a guitarist entertains shoppers outside Loot, a home furnishing and antique shop at 720 North High Street opened in 1988 by Phyllis Potts and her two daughters, Jennifer Dennis and Leslie Welsh. (Courtesy of the Columbus Metropolitan Library/ Columbus in Historic Photographs.)

The Doo Dah Parade, an Independence Day tradition, began in the Short North in 1984. Funding problems and an overly exuberant use of water guns and water balloons sidelined the parade for three years in the mid-1990s, but it has remained a popular holiday event since. These 1991 photographs feature the "Fashion Police" (at left) handing out tickets to those committing attire-related faux pas and the popular Marching Fidels (below), who are moving, as always, to the left. The parade, held every July 4, begins at Goodale Park and meanders through the streets of Victorian Village before ending on North High Street. No registration is required; participants just show up if they want to be part of the parade. The rain date is always July 3. (Both, courtesy of the author.)

This photograph of the east side of North High Street between Fourth and Fifth Avenues was taken around 1991. Dave and Linda's Carryout and Deli, owned by David and Linda Gessells, occupied 1180 North High Street for most of the 1990s. Next door, Wayne Washburn and David Sims ran Wayne's Rod and Custom Accessories, an auto parts store. (Courtesy of Columbus Metropolitan Library/Department of Development Collection.)

Global Gallery opened in 1991 at 682 North High Street. Area churches wanted to provide a nonprofit marketplace for third-world folk art and handicrafts while raising awareness about fair trade. The High Street location is shown here in 1993; Global Gallery opened other locations, and the Short North shop closed in 2014. It was replaced by Global Gifts. (Courtesy of the Columbus Metropolitan Library/Columbus in Historic Photographs.)

The Roy G. Biv gallery has been a strong supporter of innovative contemporary art since its founding in 1989. It operated out of various locations in the Short North, including the exhibit space at 714 North High Street, shown here in 1993, most likely during a Gallery Hop. In 2019, Roy G. Biv relocated to Franklinton. (Courtesy of the Columbus Metropolitan Library/Columbus in Historic Photographs.)

The Russian Tea Room, also known as the Matreoshka Russian Tea Room, was an early restaurant in the Short North. It was opened in 1986 by Anna Shriftman and her mother, Elena Kaplunovsky, and operated for a decade before it permanently closed. This picture is from 1993. (Courtesy of the Columbus Metropolitan Library/Columbus in Historic Photographs.)

In this 1993 photograph, "Gallery Hoppers" pause to look at the "Trains" mural on the south exterior wall of the Union Station Café. Painted by Gregory Ackers in 1989, it was a reminder of the stream of locomotives that once made daily stops at the nearby old Union Station. The mural disappeared during the construction of Le Méridien Columbus, The Joseph hotel. (Courtesy of the Columbus Metropolitan Library/Columbus in Historic Photographs.)

ComFest, short for "Community Festival," began near The Ohio State University campus in 1972. A decade later, the annual "party with a purpose" moved to a parking lot across from Goodale Park. A few years later, it moved into the park. The three-day, noncorporate festival blends music, arts, and political activism. Thomas Jefferson Slave Apartments is shown here performing on the Bozo Stage in 1995. (Courtesy of the author.)

This 1996 photograph shows 765 Summit Street, which has been home to various businesses, including J&J Carryout, Forby's Market, and Hazel's Confectionery. Built in 1889, the building's corner tower with the pyramidal roof is an eye-catcher. The Columbus Landmarks Foundation awarded it a 1999 James B. Recchie Design Award in the open category for "good design for the sheer pleasure it imparts." (Courtesy of Columbus Metropolitan Library/Department of Development Collection.)

Ground was broken in 1993 for the Victorian Gate apartment and condominium project between North High and Park Streets north of West Russell Street. It replaced a crater-filled parking lot with an $11 million residential and retail complex. This view from 1996 looks east on West Russell Street. (Courtesy of Columbus Metropolitan Library/Department of Development Collection.)

One never knows what might pop up in the Doo Dah Parade as it winds its way through the neighborhood every Fourth of July. Political and social satire are annual constants. In this 1998 image, the Viagra Drill Team pauses to show off a choreographed routine. (Courtesy of the author.)

The world survived Y2K as the calendar flipped from 1999 to 2000. This view from around 2:00 a.m. on January 1, 2000, shows the survivors of the New Year's Eve show at Little Brothers, located at 1100 North High Street. Local rockers Watershed headlined the concert that also included the Wahoos and the Lilybandits. (Courtesy of the author.)

The Interstate 670 reconstruction was well underway when this photograph was taken on June 23, 2002. The Park Street bridge over the interstate had been removed two months before. The 18-month project, which cost over $200 million, resulted in a direct connection between Interstate 70 on the west and Interstate 270 on the east. This view looks northeast and includes the south gate to Goodale Park. (Courtesy of the author.)

This view looks northeast over the reconstruction of Interstate 670 and construction of the North High Street Cap. The photograph was taken on February 28, 2003, and features the most southern arch over North High Street. When it was completed, the Cap mended a hole in the urban landscape between downtown and the Short North. (Courtesy of the author.)

The North High Street Cap officially opened on October 12, 2004, two months after this photograph was taken. The 26,000-square-foot cap contains shops and restaurants and fills an infrastructure gap. David Meleca, architect of the Cap, was inspired by the Beaux-Arts style of the old Union Station arcade that once stood nearby on North High Street. (Courtesy of the author.)

This photograph was taken on February 6, 2006, and looks northeast at the intersection of North High and Lincoln Streets. The picture features the iconic Short North Gothic mural painted by Mike Altmas and Steve Galgas in June 2002. North of the mural is the 11-story Bollinger Tower at 750 North High Street, an apartment building for senior citizens. (Courtesy of the author.)

This view from 2006 looks north from Poplar Avenue on North High Street. It features several of the 17 steel arches installed over the street in 2002. Problems with the lights inside the arches began soon after the initial switch was flipped. It was not until 2007, when the fiber optics were replaced by a light-emitting diode system, that the problems appeared to be solved. (Courtesy of the author.)

The bust of Lincoln Goodale near the southeast entrance to the park that bears his name is sometimes adorned with seasonal clothing items. Around Christmas, he can be spotted wearing a red-and-white Santa hat. In this 2007 picture, he is letting his freak flag fly during ComFest. (Courtesy of the author.)

The Wonder Bread Bakery at 697 North Fourth Street closed in 2009 after nearly a century of operation. It opened in 1913 under the name Columbus Bread Company. The iconic Wonder Bread sign, shown here in 2009, continues to stand at the southeast corner of Hamlet and Warren Streets as a reminder of a slice of Italian Village history. (Courtesy of the author.)

Deb Roberts has gone by many names since she first became involved with the Doo Dah Parade in 1999: Queen of Doo Dah, Mz Doo Dah, and the Doo Dah ChairChick. One constant is her devotion to the craziness and lunacy that makes up the annual Independence Day celebration. She is pictured here in 2012 wearing a tiara and a thrift-store gown. (Courtesy of the author.)

You never know what you will see in the Short North. The undead gathered in Goodale Park on May 12, 2012, for the sixth annual Zombiewalk Columbus. The charity event benefitted different organizations each year. When an estimated 4,000 people participated in 2012, canned goods were collected for the Mid-Ohio Foodbank, and cash donations were given to the Leukemia and Lymphoma Society. (Courtesy of the author.)

This view looks south on High Street and features Le Méridien Columbus, the Joseph hotel under construction in 2014. The 10-story, 135-room boutique hotel opened in early 2015. It was developed by Ron and Joel Pizzuti as part of a larger Short North complex that includes an office building and art museum. The Joseph was named for Ron's father, Joseph Pizzuti. (Courtesy of the author.)

Since 1981, the Columbus Pride Parade has been a welcoming, inclusive event. Pictured here in 2016 at the corner of North High Street and Buttles Avenue is the Columbus Gay Men's Chorus float, one of 215 entries. Grand marshal Lana Moore, a retired Columbus firefighter who is transgender, told the *Columbus Dispatch* that the event was about "love, getting along and how we treat each other." (Courtesy of the author.)

The Doo Dah Parade's banner, which reads "The End" but usually appears at the beginning of the parade, is shown here in 1999 at the corner of Neil and Wilber Avenues. A Columbus police officer typically drives the route ahead of the parade, proclaiming, "What's behind me is anyone's guess!" The Doo Dah Parade has much in common with the neighborhood through which it circulates—although the people lining the streets may not know what's coming, they know it's going to be fun and interesting, and they're probably going to like it! (Courtesy of the author.)

Visit us at
arcadiapublishing.com

www.ingramcontent.com/pod-product-compliance
Lightning Source LLC
Chambersburg PA
CBHW060938170426
43194CB00027B/2990